Successful Persuasion: I Saw it on the Radio

Gerry Borreggine

Canadian Cataloguing in Publication Data

Borreggine, Gerry, 1955-
Successful persuasion

Includes index.
ISBN 1-55212-334-0

1. Persuasion (Rhetoric) 2. Public speaking I. Title.
PE1431.B67 2000 808.5'1 C00-910092-X

TRAFFORD

This book was published *on-demand* in cooperation with Trafford Publishing.
On-demand publishing is a unique process and service of making a book available for retail sale to the public taking advantage of on-demand manufacturing and Internet marketing. **On-demand publishing** includes promotions, retail sales, manufacturing, order fulfilment, accounting and collecting royalties on behalf of the author.

Suite 6E - 2333 Government St., Victoria, B.C. V8T 4P4, CANADA
Phone 250-383-6864 Toll-free 1-888-232-4444 (Canada & US)
Fax 250-383-6804 E-mail sales@trafford.com
Web site www.trafford.com TRAFFORD PUBLISHING IS A DIVISION OF TRAFFORD HOLDINGS LTD.
Trafford Catalogue #99-0084 www.trafford.com/robots/99-0084.html

10 9 8 7 6 5

To my wife, Regina,
my daughter, Kristin,
and my son, Kyle, who all
tolerated my madness and musings
while I wrote this book.

Also, to my parents, Frank and Marie Borreggine,
who gave me the foundation to learn
whatever it is that I do know today.

TABLE OF CONTENTS

PREFACE

Perhaps at one time or another, you've been engaged in a conversation in which you were overwhelmed, if not mesmerized, by the persuasive power of the speaker. Some people seem to have an uncanny knack for being convincingly eloquent.

Have you ever thought, "If only *I* had the ability to be convincing and powerfully persuasive?" If so, this book will help you achieve that goal.

In most cases, persuasive people were not born with the ability to be so fluently eloquent. Usually, persuasive skills have been achieved through frequent application of specific communication techniques, that have been mastered over a period of time.

This book will guide you through a series of lessons that teach you how to achieve successful persuasion.

It presents you with valuable information that shows you how to establish, increase, and eventually perfect your own native ability to be a convincing and persuasive communicator.

Its subtitle, *I Saw It On The Radio*, is a graphic illustration of how different people communicate differently. It was drawn from an actual conversation that I had with a very visual-type person who communicated in pictorial terms. His description of a baseball game, that he listened to on the radio, was transferred to a vivid picture account when he recalled the game's events. By his own description, he claimed that he *saw* the game on the radio.

This information, and the lessons that surround it, construct a foundation for you to establish an understanding of how to identify the different types of communicators and then to establish an amazing rapport with them. The rapport you create allows you to become a powerfully persuasive communicator.

I am grateful to all of the persuasive teachers who have inspired my work, most especially to: Zig Ziglar, master salesman, persuasive speaker extrordinaire and author of *See You at the Top*; Dr. Kerry L. Johnson, author of *Subliminal Selling Skills*; Napoleon Hill, author of *Think and Grow Rich!*; and Dr. Norman Vincent Peale, author of *The Power of Positive Thinking*.

However, the unique aspects of this work have come from my many years on the retail sales floor of the successful company, which I am president of today, 40 Winks Sleep Shops. It was there that the guidelines in this book were established, practiced, and perfected.

I have collected the information that I have studied, practiced, perfected, and presented it in this book so that you too can achieve successful persuasion. For lasting results, ingest the information contained slowly, so that you may effectively absorb it and transfer it to your own personality.

It is my sincere belief that this information will inspire you with fresh and productive ideas on how to increase your own innate persuasive ability. Each lesson concentrates on specific areas of persuasion. Study! Read! Practice! And, eventually master the lessons one at a time. If you do this with a determined diligence, I guarantee you ***Successful Persuasion*** in all areas of your life.

LESSON ONE

Sold – on you

All over the world, in the course of communication between two people, a sale is either made or lost during the exchange of dialogue.

That's right. Think about it.

You're standing there talking to somebody and you either buy or don't buy what they're saying. You make a judgment not only about the person speaking, but also about what they are saying.

For example: Suppose there is a handsome man who's been courting a beautiful young woman for several months. The young fellow decides to make his pitch and asks the woman to be his wife. When he's finished with his presentation, it is now the young woman's turn. She either buys and says yes, or passes on the offer and says no.

She makes a decision not only on the young man, but she makes a decision about what the young fellow has said to her. She either buys it, or she doesn't. It's really that simple.

She says yes and a sale has been made. Or she says no and there is a cancellation, or a no-sale is registered. During the exchange, a decision is made.

These exchanges go on everyday, be it at the market, at school, at work, or even at home. There is a sale to be made or lost in every conversation. Those sales, or lost sales, are decided upon the persuasiveness and the credibility of the participants doing the conversing.

The big question, of course, that will be asked by many is: How can I become one of those persuasive people?

For some, that talent may come quite naturally. Others, however, will find that perfecting the skill of persuasive communication is a laborious effort that will be difficult to master. The pages which lie ahead will detail various strategies that will help the reader achieve a persuasive persona. Many of the techniques described will focus on building rapport with your conversational rival.

It is the basic premise of this book that your persuasiveness will increase in direct proportion with your ability to build rapport. Following this principle will put you directly on the road to success when engaged in conversational communication.

Also, possessing the ability to identify persuasive speaking skills will afford you the luxury of accurately drawing objective conclusions on the subject matter, without being excessively influenced by the persuasive speaking techniques that are being employed by the speaker. You'll find that your ability to identify these communication techniques will put you in position to separate the wheat from the chaff in the speaker's dialogue and presentation.

An additional benefit that will be derived from this knowledge will be the acquired ability to distinguish fact from fiction in many verbal exchanges. During many conversations, decisions are made and ideas are formulated on false and erroneous information. The information expelled by either one or more of the parties is deliberately false, but it is portended to be true.

During these deliberately false exchanges, one party has attempted to convince, or colloquially speaking, *bullshit*, the other into believing the false statements they have made are actually true.

Will this book be able to provide the answer to the ages, that is, finding the truth?

If only if it were that simple.

If everything you've ever heard were the unequivocal truth, what a simple life this would be.

There would be no fear of ever being wrong or hoodwinked.

When your children tell you that they didn't do it...they didn't.

When your friend tells you that you look terrific...you do.

And when the car salesman tells you that the model you are looking at was driven by a little old lady who only used the car to get back and forth to church on Sunday...it's gospel!

That, we all know, is far from the truth and it rarely, if ever, happens. We're lied to, hoodwinked, and blatantly bullshitted on a daily basis. In most cases, we don't even know it when this does occur to us.

There's no tome that has ever been written or recorded that would distinguish fact from fiction for its audience. This book will not attempt to be any different in that regard.

However, if it can enlighten you, the reader, to see through even just one attempt to mislead or bullshit you, I guarantee you that these pages will be worth the price you paid for them many times over.

And, if it affords you the ability to present your thoughts or words in a manner that your audience will find irresistibility persuasive, then there'll be one less person in this world that you will need to convince about your prevailing power – you!

LESSON TWO

Some people say it walks

"Money talks, bullshit walks."

There may not exist an old adage, or expression, that is more convoluted than that.

Ostensibly, to the hip-talking speaker, this bold statement probably means something like, "If you don't have the money, take a hike because talk is cheap."

But, if you're ever looking for an opportunity to win in a negotiation situation – or to pull a fast one – the person who makes the above proclamation, is probably your best target.

What an overstated exclamation of false bravado, "Money talks, bullshit walks."

I've never seen money do anything but change hands.

Bullshit, however, has proven itself to be a much more versatile commodity. In fact there is a germ of truth in half of that infected statement. Bullshit does walk – away *with* the money!

A red flag should go up inside your head, immediately, when you hear someone make that statement. That speaker is either badly insecure about themself, to the point that they need to make a bold, and most likely inaccurate, statement about their ability to separate fact from fiction; or you're about to be tipped-off that the speaker is one grossly overconfident individual who's quite prone to be duped.

A genuinely secure and confident speaker would never need to feed their own ego by telling you how wise or savvy they are, nor would they tip their hand to expose their own confidence.

These are cards that are always to be kept close to the vest.

The same goes double for the individual who utters the statement, "Never bullshit a bullshitter," when referring to their own persuasive prowess.

It is the ultimate declaration of conversational pomposity.

If ever there is anyone who is begging to be taken advantage of, it is the unfortunate dupe who makes this overwhelming statement falsely bragging of their ability.

LESSON THREE

The home-field advantage

A cardinal rule in negotiating is to conduct discussions on your own turf, or the place of *your* choice. You want to be at a place where you are familiar and comfortable.

Conversely, avoid encounters which allow the negotiations to occur at a place that is the choice of your opponent. If this does occur, you're relinquishing what could be a very valuable home-field advantage.

While winning and losing aren't solely determined by who possesses the home-field advantage, the benefit of conducting discussions at your determined location could provide you with the added margin necessary for victory.

Let's examine this home-field advantage as it applies to sports – football in particular.

Using the 1993 year as our model and the National Football League and its twenty-eight teams as our sample, the mean-average winning percentage for that year was fifty percent. That is, according to the *Sporting News*, during the 1993 season there were 224 games played and in every contest, there was one winner and one loser.

However, the overall home-field record, for the games played in which the home team's winning percentage is computed, was fifty-four point nine percent.

That means that in the NFL, the home team has an almost five percent better chance of winning than does the visiting team. That five percent doesn't take any other factors into consideration, such as disparity of quality between the teams, injured players, or extraneous elements such as weather. It's an outright five percent advantage just for being the home team!

Why would something as simple as a home-field advantage produce such positive results for the home team?

First of all, there's a significant degree of success created by working in comfortable and familiar surroundings. On the other hand, there's an equal amount of anxiety and even discomfort created for those who are operating on unfamiliar turf.

On your home turf you're in control of much of the situation, such as where the discussion takes place, the time it takes place, and where you sit or stand during the discussion.

Your opponent, however, is in control of none of these matters. They've been placed in the position of being the guest, and by observing even general rules of social graces, they must respectfully acquiesce to your wishes. In this case, it may be the first of many concessions they'll be making during the course of discussions.

Once you've gotten your opponent to make that first concession, to meet you at the place of *your* choice, they'll be more likely to make even more concessions. Get your opponent to agree where to meet you and you've won the first round of the battle.

If you're looking to avoid being out-maneuvered, stay in a comfortable setting where you are more likely to maintain control of the situation.

Make your opponent work harder and make it increasingly difficult for them to achieve a degree of comfort during negotiations by forcing them to be the visitor or the "away team."

Negotiate on a home field. You'll have the wind at your back, and your opponent will be swimming upstream from the start.

LESSON FOUR

Sizing-up the competition

To be an effective communicator, and a successful one at that, you must know and understand your opposition.

However, one of the most important objectives in effective communication is to build rapport with your opponent. Your ability to persuade an opponent will increase in direct proportion to this.

The more you know about your opponent, the easier it will be for you to build rapport.

There is a old, Italian expression brought to this country by the immigrants who arrived in America early in the twentieth century, which emphasizes the previous point: "Keep your friends close to you, but keep your enemies closer."

There are many ways in which to build this connection and many will be discussed in the chapters that lie ahead. However, if you are able to size-up your opponent and understand his mode of communication, you'll find it much easier to build rapport and, subsequently, devise a plan of attack in pursuing a course of communication.

It is important to speak to your opponent in the manner in which he prefers to communicate.

What does that mean?

Well, if you can identify the mode of communication in which your opponent communicates, and you can respond, in kind, to that type of communication, you will find it much easier to be persuasive.

Dr. Kerry L. Johnson, author of *Subliminal Selling Skills*, wrote about the researchers at the University of California at Santa Cruz who studied the manner in which people think and communicate in order to help therapists deal more effectively in resolving psychological problems. The researchers, a linguist and a psycho-therapist, spent years looking at the process by which patients and clients used language, and the thought process behind the use of that language.

The researchers discovered that people think and communicate in three basic modes. They identified three distinctly different groups of people who both think and communicate in one of these identified modes.

They established one group as the *visuals*. These are the people who transmit and receive information primarily through a visual or picture sense. As these people receive information, they are making pictures or snapshots in their mind of exactly what's being received by them. When speaking, these people often graphically describe their own thoughts to their audience.

They established another group as the *auditories*. These are people who are likely to listen intently to what is being said. They respond to sound. What they hear and how they hear it is very important to them.

The third group was labeled as the *kinesthetics*. These are the people who are the touchy-feely type. They respond the strongest to gut or visceral feelings. They are the type most likely to get goose-bumps if they can grasp a situation.

The researchers found that most people, if not all, have a primary mode of communication in which they are the most comfortable and familiar. This isn't to say that visuals, for example, will only communicate visually, or that auditories only receive and transmit information auditorily. It's just that for most people, one mode is their natural, or what I'll call, their home-base mode of communication.

If you can identify this home-base mode of your opponent, chances are, you'll find it easier to chart a course of attack in devising a verbal assault against your opponent.

If it does turn out that your opponent is a visual, and you begin to communicate to them in visual terms, you'll find that building rapport and enhancing your own persuasiveness will increase dramatically.

The advantage to be gained when you can identify your opponent's home-base mode gives you such an overwhelming edge in communication, it's almost unfair!

When you have identified your opponent's natural mode, you've begun to unlock the mystery of how their subconscious mind operates.

By using subliminal techniques, you'll appeal to your opponent in a very persuasive manner – through their subconscious mind.

Subliminal communication techniques being utilized by you to increase your persuasiveness and overcome your opponent?

Wow, it sounds like the stuff of the CIA and KGB.

And you are going to employ these techniques in your interactions with everyday people?

It almost sound illegal.

But, it isn't.

LESSON FIVE

The eyes have it!

Identifying the home-base mode of the person who you are dealing with may be easier than you think it is.

In fact, soon after your initial meeting, you may be tipped-off as to just what type of person you are confronting, merely by watching the eye movements of your subject.

The researches at Santa Cruz became fascinated with something called neurolinguistic psychology which, in layman terms, is the study of the relationship between eye movement and behavior. Useful insights about people became apparent and have proved to be quite helpful in predicting human behavior, especially when the research was applied to practical interactive conversations.

Simply put, the way a person's eyes move, or are positioned, can provide you with valuable clues about the thoughts and the psychological reaction of that person to what you're saying. It can also alert you as to what is that person's natural mode of communication.

A *visual* person will often move their eyes *up to the right* and *up to the left* while they are receiving information. Since this person thinks in picture form, they're drawing images in their mind as you speak to them. They will focus up to the left or up to the right, contemplating the images they're making as they receive information from you.

This person also will sometimes stare directly at the ceiling as they're picturing just what it is you're saying to them. A smile following this contemplation is usually a sign that they've just assimilated the information they've received, and they understand it.

In less frequent instances, the visual will sometimes stare blankly straight ahead with their eyes in an unfocused position. Again, this is the mode in which they receive the message and translate it into picture form within their mind.

However, if the unfocused eye movement continues for a prolonged period or even after you've delivered your message, your subject has probably lost interest in your discourse. This person now may be passively receiving your information, and no longer concentrating on the substance of your words. At this point, you can no longer use eye movement as a barometer to identify your subject's home-base mode of communication. Here, it's time to reload and start again, preferably after you have engaged your subject in some response to what you have said. It may be wise to relinquish the floor for a matter of time, while you allow your subject the opportunity to speak. Use this time to reformulate a new plan of attack.

Auditories often will position their eyes *down to the left* as they receive information. This is the concentration mode for these people. They're pensively contemplating as they receive verbal input. Auditories, also, will often move their eyes *side right to side left* as they receive information. This may happen when information is being presented in a rapid-fire pace, when the information received is exciting to them, or is of high interest. The excitement of the message will register in their eyes as they quickly move back and forth to each side of their head as they listen intently.

Kinesthetics will often move their eyes *down to the right* as they receive information. As they concentrate on the message received, they're relating to the tactile sensations of what it is that's being said. These kinesthetics are visceral people who are imagining the *feeling* of what's being communicated. It's important to try to give these people first-hand experience with what is being spoken.

It will take much practice and careful concentration in dealing with your subjects to understand and perfect these techniques. It will not come easy. You'll have to persist and continue to practice them in your everyday encounters with people. However, as you continue to study them, you'll find many reoccurring situations that will help you to identify the home-base mode of the person you are studying. After awhile, it will become easier for you, and soon, before you even recognize it, you will be subconsciously sizing-up and identifying people.

While learning to perfect your skills, there is one caveat of which you should be aware. Do not make long and uncomfortable eye contact with people while you are trying to determine their mode type.

These people do not know what you're doing and they might think you are crazy, or something even worse.

While you try to identify them, they'll be thinking, "Why is this person staring at me?…Is this person on drugs?…Is there something hanging off my face?"

You're trying too hard if you give your subject reason to think something is up, let alone allowing them to imagine that something is wrong.

Be discreet. Use casual glances aimed at their eye movements immediately after you've made a statement. Give them, and their eyes, a chance to respond.

LESSON SIX

The visuals

As you speak to a visual person, their brain works similarly to how a language translator's mind operates. But instead of translating from one language to another, the visual's brain translates the language spoken from words to pictures. The words which the visual receives are transformed to related snapshots in their mind that they can view and access with relative ease.

Visuals also speak in picture form. They try to describe the pictures that they see in their minds to the people with whom they're communicating.

In addition to their eye movements, their words are an easy clue as to what type of communicator they are.

"I *see* what you are saying."

"It *looks* like rain today."

"I get the *picture*."

"I can *envision* that."

"I'll *show* you what I mean."

The words that they use tell you exactly that these are picture-type, or visual people.

And who are these visual people?

There are some obvious examples of who might be a visual, such as a painter, an artist, a photographer, or an interior decorator. But, others may also be visuals. Some are people you'd least expect. It could be your accountant, your mailman, or even your best friend.

My wife and I had an experience of coming in contact with a visual-type person a few years ago. Unfortunately, at that time, neither one of us knew anything about neurolinguistic psychology or identifying the home-base mode of people during the course of communicating.

We had decided to build a sun-room addition to our house. We interviewed several builders for the job. One contractor, who came highly recommended, failed to impress us during the interview process. In fact, he actually irritated us by acting in, what we perceived to be, an aloof and distant manner.

As we spoke, he often looked away in what appeared to be a blank stare. He very rarely made eye contact with either one of us. When we told him what we wanted in this room, his eyes would move up and to the right. We didn't realize it at the time, but he was apparently visualizing how our plans would look as an addition to our house. His eyes were looking to the future, formulating a picture as to how this building would appear.

When we asked him how the addition would blend in with the existing frame of our house, he paused, and his eyes went up and to the right. Then he replied, "I *see* us using a gable roof to match the existing lines of the house."

It wasn't until he first pictured the addition and then described it to us, that his eyes returned to us for a response.

Despite the fact that my wife and I didn't feel comfortable with our visual contractor, we decided to have him do the work for us, anyway. There was something that we liked about him, although, at the time, we were unable to identify it. As it turned out, we judged him correctly. He did a wonderful job and built a splendid addition to our house.

A few years later, we decided to have additional work done to our house. By now, we were aware of neurolinguistic psychology, and this time we had identified our contractor to be a definite visual-type person.

When our contractor friend didn't make eye contact with us during discussions, we smiled confidently. We knew he was imaging how our plans would look in the work he would be doing for us. In fact, we'd often pause during the conversation to allow him to form exact pictures of what we wanted him to build for us.

Also, since we knew him to be a definite visual, we spoke to him in a visual context, that is, a language of graphic pictures. We spoke to the *angles* we wanted in the room, the *view* we wanted the room to have from the other rooms in the house, and the *look* we wanted the addition to have from the street.

We knew we were building rapport with our contractor, because after he pictured what we described to him, he smiled. He understood us!

I vividly remember his response to our plan, "I *see* what you're *looking* for."

The number of people who are like our contractor friend that use the visual mode as their home base of communication is about thirty-five percent.

These visuals are easy to build rapport with if you can get them to visualize pictures and snapshots in their mind while you're speaking to them.

Say you want to go to the baseball game tomorrow and you want your visual friend to come along. You want them to imagine the good things that they would enjoy if they agreed to go.

"Can't you just *imagine* us taking the day off tomorrow to *watch* an afternoon baseball game?" Here the visual pictures the events that will take place if they go to the game. They imagine the vivid green turf, the view of the stadium, the hot dogs, the peanuts, and the beer. If you get the visual to do this, you've got yourself a partner at tomorrow's game. Get them making pictures and get their eyes viewing those pictures of the future.

This quick study of a visuals's eye movements can actually give you a good idea if the visual person, with whom you're communicating, is telling you the truth.

In his book, *Subliminal Selling Skills*, Dr. Kerry Johnson tells of how the FBI train their agents in an easy technique to help the agents determine fact from fiction with the people they confront. FBI agents can't give everyone they meet a lie detector test, so they teach their agents the basics of neurolinguistic psychology to determine if people are telling them the truth.

You see, when a visual pictures the future, their eyes move up and to the right. They're constructing a photo in their brain of something they're envisioning, or they are imaging the future. However, when a visual moves their eyes up and to the left, they are reviewing a previously constructed image, or recalling past photos contained in their mind.

Now, here you are face-to-face with a visual-type person. You ask them a question about something that occurred last week. They pause, collect their thoughts, and their eyes move up and to the right as they begin to speak. They're imaging photos in front of them, images that are in their future, not images that were in their past.

Since you asked about a previous experience, the visual should've been recalling those past photos, not imaging new photos of the future.

If this visual was telling the truth, then when they went to recall the past, their eyes should've moved up and to the left to revisit those previous images. Instead, they looked up and to the right, to the future, and they constructed new pictures. Or, you could say, they constructed a lie. They didn't review past events, they created new events when recalling something that had previously occurred. Simply put, they lied.

Imagine how helpful this knowledge is to the FBI when they confront a foreign envoy. Without electronic testing devises, these well-trained agents can actually identify fact from fiction – all by studying eye movements!

If you want to build rapport, and ultimately get a visual person to agree with you, speak to them in the manner they want to be spoken to – visually.

When dealing with them, try to get that little slide projector in their brain clicking away. If they can formulate pictures of the words you send them, they'll understand you better. If they understand you, you will find it easy to build rapport with them.

Once you do identify a person to be this photo-frame thinking visual, you will see that speaking to them in their language will allow you to substantially increase your own persuasiveness in your dealings with them.

LESSON SEVEN

The auditories

The auditory is the type of person who may be the easiest to communicate with. If you speak to them properly, they'll listen intently to what you say.

They will not only be listening to your words, but they'll also be listening to the sounds of your words. The timbre, the inflection, the pace, the pronunciation, and even the manner itself in which the words are communicated are all important to them.

Where the visual's mind was described to work like a slide projector that accessed both past and future photos, the auditory's mind works like a tape recorder. It, also, will access both past and present experiences, but it does so in the form of conversations that either *have* taken place, or conversations that they imagine *will* take place.

If you ask an auditory to recall a specific event, they'll first recall the conversation or the words that were associated with that event. Even when dealing with a future event, the auditory will relate to it in the form of words.

"I wonder what my boss will *say* when I *tell* him I got the order?"

Or, "I can't wait to *hear* what my wife's going to say when I *tell* her I got a raise."

The auditory's specific eye movements will help you to identify the type of person he or she is. Eyes that move down and to the left identifies a person to be an auditory.

When an auditory's eyes move down and to the left, they're contemplating the information they are receiving. When you see the person you're speaking to position their eyes down and to the left, you can be sure that this person is thinking auditorily.

When the auditory moves their eyes down and to the left, they're seriously considering what you've just said to them. In some cases, when they move their eyes to this position, you may even find this person speaking to themselves. It is at this point that you should stop talking and allow the auditory to finish the debate raging inside them.

Side-to-side eye movement also indicates that you're dealing with an auditory. Similarly, as with visuals, this side-to-side movement may occur as rapid-eye movement when an auditory is presented with words or conversation at a rapid pace, or sounds that illicit a strong or passionate response.

When an auditory moves their eyes side right, they're looking to the future as to what conversation might take place in the scene they're contemplating.

"I wonder what my kids will *say* when they *hear* I got tickets for tonight's circus?"

When the auditory's eyes move side left, they're recalling a previous conversation that had taken place.

"I remember what my boss *said* the last time I *asked* him for the weekend off."

But, you will find the auditory's words to be their most distinguishing trait. The predicates they use when speaking are distinctly based in their most comfortable mode of communication.

"That *sounds* good to me."

"I *hear* what you're saying."

"*Listen* to this..."

"That *rings* a bell."

"Don't use that *tone* on me."

"I would like to *voice* my concerns."

"I *hear* you *loud and clear.*"

Like the visuals, once you identify an auditory and you speak to them in the manner which they want to be spoken to, auditorily, you'll build rapport and increase your own persuasiveness with them immensely.

If the language you speak is *in concert* with that of the auditory mind, you will strike a *chord* with that auditory person that will *ring* true to their soul.

Again, like visuals, these auditories can be almost anyone. But as you can imagine, some people are more likely to be auditories than are others.

Linguists, musicians, and recording artists are people who would typically be auditories.

I had a music professor in college who was a good example of an auditory.

When asked how he was inspired to write the music which he would present to the class for study, this professor said that he would hear the individual voices in the class performing their part of the music, which he would be composing at the piano, as he was actually writing it.

He would then come into class and describe the completed sound he heard inside his head, and how he intended to blend the classes' voices with musical instruments he planned to use. He sometimes would describe, in detail, a sound which he had not yet even written. It was just that his mind communicated in specific sounds – musical sounds.

His listening ability was so acute that he would hear the slightest or smallest mistake in the rehearsals. He would have the class repeat their performance until every voice and every instrument was perfect.

I remember one particular class where we were working on an especially complex arrangement. When we finished, the entire class was proud and happy with the performance, except our professor. He heard something he didn't like and had us repeat it. I remember remarking to a fellow classmate, "This guy can hear sounds that not even a dog could detect!"

Obviously, not everybody will be as extreme of an example of an auditory as my college professor. But with a little attention to detail, you will be able to identify these people.

Whereas, about thirty-five percent of the people will be visuals, only twenty-five percent of the population will turn out to be auditories. These auditories are the smallest of the three different types of people we will study.

They identify themselves by their eye movements and by the words they use when they are communicating. They will respond the best when you communicate to them in a manner which pays careful attention to the words and sounds you present to them.

Try to be as articulate and precise in what you say and how you say it when speaking to them. They are the type of people who will be thrown-off by a mispronounced word or a discordant-sounding conversation.

They are the people who are likely to sometimes talk to themselves. No, they aren't crazy. But yes, they are inclined to have inner conversations with that tape recorder inside their head.

These auditories are good storytellers. They like to both tell and hear stories during the course of conversation. Allow them to tell you their stories. And, reply to them with story examples or your own.

Also, auditories are good telephone people. They seem to communicate especially well over the phone, conducting business and even relationships there.

Remember to talk to them the way they want to be spoken to. Keep your conversations moving smoothly when you converse with these people.

Talk to them in sounds, and they will listen to you intently.

LESSON EIGHT

The kinesthetics

The kinesthetics are the touchy-feely type of people who make decisions based on how they *feel* about the information they're receiving. Their opinions are often based on the visceral or gut-feelings they get about people or information.

They form opinions based on touch, feel, emotion, and attitude. They're likely to get goose-bumps when they sense something that will illicit a strong emotional response.

These kinesthetics have minds that operate much like the little old lady in the produce section of the supermarket – the one who has to touch and feel all the fruit and vegetables before she decides to buy any of it.

These kinesthetics respond to certain feelings they get when they're receiving information. They, also, are the largest of the three groups of people we have discussed. They comprise of about forty percent of the people you will meet.

The kinesthetics formulate their opinions quickly as their initial impressions about something or someone will play heavily in their decisions on that subject. They are the people that are most likely to make quick decisions.

It is important that you are especially careful in your dealings with these people.

Try to appeal to the sense of what they feel strongly about. Reinforce the positive feelings that the kinesthetics have declared to be their strong, emotional contact-points.

When the kinesthetic receives information or contemplates what has just been said, you will find their basic eye movement to be down and to the right. It is when their eyes are in this position that they are gathering their feelings on the subject at hand. They attempt to *get a hold of* their *feelings* to help them *form* opinions.

The kinesthetics may be the most difficult type of people to deal with because their emotions play such an important role in their decision making process. It is important to stay objective in your own thinking process when dealing with them. However, while doing this, try to appeal to the subjective nature of the kinesthetic mind.

Like the visual and the auditory, the words the kinesthetics use when communicating will help you to identify them.

"*Touch* base with me in the morning."

"I have a good *grasp* of what's been said."

"That *rubs* me the wrong way."

"I *feel* good about today's meeting."

"I'm *comfortable* with that idea."

"I'll try to *get hold of* you tomorrow."

As mentioned earlier, Dr. Kerry Johnson is a psychologist who has done extensive research in the field of neuro-linguistic psychology, decision strategies, and even subliminal seduction in advertising. Much of Johnson's work is concentrated on sales related applications. However, he has done extensive work in studying athletes and related sports psychology.

Johnson has determined that many athletes are kinesthetics. They love the *feeling* they get from winning.

He uses a famous ice hockey player, Wayne Gretzky, as an example of a pure kinesthetic.

Gretzky is hockey's most prolific scorer. His performance on the ice has shattered just about every record in the sport. His scoring output has been almost double that of even his closest competitor in nearly every season he's played.

Johnson described that in interviewing Gretzky, he asked him what it was that made him such a gifted scorer.

Gretzky replied that when he was around the net with the puck on his hockey stick, he'd get a certain *feeling* to shoot the puck. And when Gretzky gets that feeling, it's usually bad news for the opposing team.

Confirming the fact that Gretzky is a kinesthetic was an observation Johnson made during his interview. He noticed that Gretzky was wearing two different colored socks.

Johnson asked Gretzky, "Gee Wayne, do you realize that you're wearing two different colored socks?"

"No, Kerry," replied Gretzky, "They're the same to me – I go by thickness!"

A kinesthetic trait, for sure, albeit an extreme one at that.

Kinesthetics do think and communicate uniquely.

When conversing, kinesthetics often make frequent pauses as they speak. They're trying to get a *feeling* about what they're hearing and, in return, they are trying to get a *handle* on how they feel they need to respond.

And, as mentioned earlier, they are the touchy-feely type. They love to touch people and things. They often will get more information from what they touch and feel than by what they see or hear. You may find that kinesthetics will touch you to make a statement or a point.

The feelings they receive and transmit are very important to them.

For example, say a kinesthetic goes out to the theater one evening. That person is less affected by the good view of the stage that they have from their seat, than they are by the comfort or discomfort of the chair, itself. The beauty of the hall has less impact on them than does the temperature of the theater. These people need to *feel comfortable.*

Also, remember, kinesthetics formulate strong opinions on initial impressions. Be aware and on-guard for that.

They will respond well to ideas and things that they can feel and touch. Allow their tactile sense to run wild when you communicate with them. Put props in their hands, pat them on the back, and allow them to touch you, in return. They need to get a good feeling about you if you're to build rapport with them. Their good feelings about you will increase your persuasiveness with kinesthetics.

If you can get the kinesthetic to *grasp* the point you make to them, you will *push* their emotional *hot-button* and they will get a *firm hold* of your idea and what you are saying to them.

LESSON NINE

Who are you?

By now everyone who has read this far is probably wondering, "What type of person am I? Am I a visual, an auditory, or a kinesthetic?"

As you may suspect, you are really a little of all three. However, one mode is your natural or comfort position. It's the mode in which you subconsciously operate. It's your home-base mode of communication.

Nearly everyone has a home-base mode. And while nearly everyone does, in fact, communicate in all three modes, their home-base mode is their subconscious favorite. It's the mode by which they are the most likely to receive information favorably.

It's in this mode that they'll find it the easiest to understand and decipher information. And, it's the home-base mode that they'll subconsciously return to, when the situation at hand allows them to think or communicate in their mode of choice.

It's also in this natural mode that people will project or transmit information with the most clarity and conviction. The subconscious mind prefers to operate in the home-base mode.

How is it that you can decide what is your own home-base mode?

Well, how is it that you think, or how is it that you construct your own thoughts?

Do you think or construct your thoughts in pictures or scenes?

Do you recall the past or imagine the future in conversations that have taken place, or conversations that you imagine will take place?

Or, do you think in tactile, sensory thoughts?

If you're still not sure. Think of an event that has recently taken place in which you were involved. What are the first and most memorable things you remember about that event?

Let's say there was a thunderstorm last night. What was it about that storm that you remember the most? Was it the flash of lightning that lit the house as it sparked the dark of night? Was it the sound of the rain pounding on your roof and window sill? Or, was it the house shaking from the crash of thunder reverberating from the sky?

Are you getting the idea?

Let's try another example. Remember the back-to-school night when you went to your child's school to become acquainted with the school and the teachers. What are the first things you remember about your surroundings of that night?

Was it the hard and uncomfortable table and chairs they had you sit in that evening? If it was, there's a good chance you could be a kinesthetic. You were responding to tactile sensations.

Was it the teacher's speech to the parents or the commanding sound of her voice that sticks out in your mind? If so, you may be an auditory who was responding to the sounds and the conversations that took place that night.

Or was it the big alphabet letters in both print and cursive that surrounded the classroom? If your mind first recalled that picture and the other graphics displayed in the room, you're probably a visual person.

Try yet another exercise. Think of everything you did this morning from the time you woke up until you had breakfast. What are the first and strongest thoughts you have about this morning?

Was it the piercing sound of the alarm clock that jostled you awake, or the soothing sounds of the birds chirping outside your window?

Was it the sun shining through your shutters and beaming into your half-opened eyes, or the television show you watched while you got dressed?

Or was it the soothing spray of the hot shower splashing on your face and warming you from head-to-toe?

As you can see, you get a pretty good idea of who or what you are just by studying how you review your own events of the day.

By now, you've probably identified yourself as one of the three types of people. While it's nice for you to know your own type, it's really much more important for you to identify the home-base mode of the people around you, or the people with whom you are communicating. Once you identify the type of person you're dealing with, you can go on with your appeal to their subconscious by communicating to them in *their* home-base mode.

The people around you will subconsciously find it very appealing and pleasing when you direct conversation to them in their natural mode of communication. You'll be appealing to them in a manner which they do not consciously identify, but do recognize, just the same, to be agreeable.

While this subconscious appeal goes virtually undetected by the person who is receiving your message, you consciously are exploiting an advantage that the person on the receiving end doesn't even know exists.

It's an advantage that will put you in the driver's seat during many a debate or conversation. It will undoubtedly increase your persuasiveness and add a distinct degree of conversational charm to your communication skills.

LESSON TEN

Listen carefully

It is critical for you to continue to develop skills that will help you build rapport.

One very important aspect of persuasive speaking for you to develop and cultivate is the skill of listening. However, it is a skill that some of the world's best speakers find difficult to master.

Why?

Well, some speakers are so intent on getting their own point across that they do not listen to what is being said to them. In some cases, the speaker is so anxious to speak their part, that when the conversing partner is talking, the speaker is not listening. Instead, they are concentrating on what they are going to say next.

As foolish as this sounds, it does occur quite often. And those over-anxious speakers are forfeiting a very valuable asset that they will need to win any debate. The asset is, listening to your opponent.

For example, let's say a car salesman is trying to sell a prospective buyer the shiny new black convertible on his showroom floor. He could have the world's best sales presentation and the most eloquent verbal delivery imaginable. But if he's not a good listener, he will not be able to sell that new car to this prospect.

Why?

Because he won't be able to overcome this potential buyer's objections.

This buyer may love the car, the style, and even the price. But, they want it in white!

The over-anxious salesman will probably miss the fact that the color of the car is really the most important part of the selection process to this buyer, who happens to be a visual.

It is very important to listen to the people with whom you converse. Listen carefully, and listen intently. You'll be surprised with what you can learn, especially when you are consciously looking for so much.

Listen to what is being said, the words communicating the thoughts, and the pace in which the words are delivered. Then, mark-out the key words these people use. These key words will help you to identify the home-base mode of communication for the people you are studying.

Take your time. Listen. Study. Then, speak on cue, but only when it is your turn to do so.

Once you get the opportunity to speak, make the most of it. Now it is your turn to shine.

But, before you employ all that you've studied and learned, there is one caveat of which you should be aware. It is the one maxim that must be understood, kept in mind, and practiced before you ever take the floor. ***Do not over-speak or over-sell yourself or your ideas!***

The byproduct of not over-selling is good listening. A good listener will be able to be precise and concise in their replies. They do not need to cover a lot of ground in their answers and conversations. They know the shortest route to the conclusion of a conversation, and they travel that road as frequently as they are able to deliver their point.

As a college student, I worked in the Television Department of a department store. I remember that selling console TV sets wasn't an easy task, but it was a very profitable one when I was successful in closing a sale. On one especially quiet night when I was working, a woman came right up to me and said, "I'll take that one."

"That one" was the most expensive TV set on the floor. One just didn't get that many people who were interested in spending $1,000 on a TV set in those days, let alone buy one at that price without even being given a sales demonstration.

I remember saying to the woman, "You've made an excellent choice, but you can't buy this television without allowing me to give you a demonstration of all its fine features."

She did not care, she just wanted to buy it. However, I persisted in my appeal to show her what a wonderful television this was.

Well, a funny thing happened. During my earnest sales demonstration, I presented one of the many fine features of the set, its automatic fine-tuning button. For whatever the reason, that feature was a problem for her. She not only didn't like it, but it upset her enthusiasm for buying the TV.

She proceeded to tell me that she now needed to go home and think about it. She was no longer sure that this was the television set she wanted in her home.

I don't remember if I was more overcome by the confusion of what had just happened, or by the grief of losing a fifty-dollar commission for selling a top-of-the-line TV set.

But I do remember the words of wisdom spoken to me by the old and seasoned salesman in the adjacent Furniture Department, who'd just watched me blow an easy one.

He said, "Kid, when they say they'll take it, just shut-up and write the order. The only thing you could do by talking after they say, 'I'll take it,' is lose the sale."

I don't remember if I actually learned the lesson that night, but I can assure you, I do recall that encounter often when I get someone to agree with me, or buy my ideas while I still have the urge to continue talking. Now, I shut-up.

An entertaining, although probably apocryphal, story about over-selling is told by master salesperson, author, and motivational speaker, Zig Ziglar in his warning to his followers to resist the temptation of over-selling themselves and their products.

In his book and tape series, *See You At The Top*, Ziglar tells the story of the Catholic girl who came home one day to tell her momma that she wanted to marry the Baptist boy that she'd been dating.

Her mother told her that, where they lived, Catholic girls just didn't marry Baptist boys. She continued to tell her daughter that if she really loved this boy and did want to marry him, she had only one choice – teach him about their religion and get him to convert to Catholicism.

The girl and the mother went to work on the boy immediately. They began to sell the boy on everything they knew and loved about their religion. They took him to church on every Sunday and holy day. They had the boy receive all the appropriate Catholic sacraments. They presented a strong and very thorough case to they boy, and soon he bought, and did convert. It wasn't that tough of a sale because, after all, the boy was already sold on the product – he loved the girl. But now, everyone was happy, and soon a wedding day was set.

For good measure, the mother and daughter continued to educate the boy about his new religion and further sold him on the aspects of being a fine Catholic.

Then, one day before the wedding, the daughter came home crying, as Zig put it, "giant crocodile tears," as she told her mother that the wedding was off.

The mother couldn't believe the news. "What happened?" she incredulously asked her daughter.

"We did everything for that boy. We took him to mass, we gave him a thorough education on church customs, we sold him on everything about the Catholic Church."

"Well momma," the girl said, "that's just the problem, we did *too* good of a job on him. He's decided to become a priest!"

By now, I'm sure you get the idea. When you've made your point and your idea has been accepted, be quiet and enjoy the victory.

You are through talking. Now get back to listening and observing so that you can be on to your next victory.

LESSON ELEVEN

Mirroring and imaging

Next on the agenda to help you develop the ability to build rapport, is the technique known as mirroring or imaging.

This mirroring is something you'll be able to employ in communications both verbally, as well as non-verbally.

From the verbal standpoint, you will mark-out key words, which are used by specific people, to help you identify what type of person it is that you're studying. As mentioned earlier, visuals, for example, will use key words or phrases that will identify them to be visual thinking people.

I once identified a person whom I was conversing with as a visual by his account of the previous night's baseball game. He recounted the game to me with a vivid description. His recollection of the game's events was so specific that I asked him if he'd attended the game in person.

"No," he said, "I *saw* it on the radio."

That statement, all by itself, spoke volumes about what type of person he was. Obviously, he'd listened to the entire game on the radio. However, his brain had transferred the announcer's description of the play-by-play to pictures and snapshots of how he imagined the events of the game that were taking place.

All three types of people will speak true to their home-base mode of communication. And you, in return, will benefit greatly if you speak to them in that defined mode.

For example, a visual person may tell you that they'd like to go to the theater with you. They tell you that they'd like tickets with a "spectacular view." First, you must define just what they mean by "spectacular view." Are they looking for front row seats that give them a close-up view, or seats in the balcony that give a panoramic view? Once that is defined, you may carry on.

When you present them the theater tickets, you mirror their phrase in your description of the tickets.

"I got the theater tickets, and they have a 'spectacular view'."

Here, you are appealing to them in a subconsciously pleasing manner by mirroring a key word or phrase that they've already marked-out as important to them. The reciting of this phrase is pleasing to them in a manner that they do not consciously recognize. It's an exact phrase that they've used in describing a desired situation, and you, in turn, have presented this phrase back to them in an attempt to gain rapport. This is an example of verbal mirroring.

When attempting to mirror your subject verbally, be sure to notice the timbre, pace, pitch, and volume at which they speak. Do your best to match those variables when addressing or answering them.

If they speak slowly at a low volume, try to do the same. If their voice comes across loud and resonating, do your best to maintain the same presence in your replies or questions back to them.

Again, your subject will find the mirror imaging of their vocal patterns to be agreeable and subconsciously pleasing to them.

This mirroring and imaging can also be effectively accomplished non-verbally, or physically. By matching your subject's body language, posture, facial expressions, and gestures, you'll be able to build rapport at a much faster rate than if you were to ignore these non-verbal clues.

The body language of your subject can tell you much about them and how they're thinking.

I work with a vendor who has the habit of taking off his eye glasses and raising the tip of his tongue to his top lip during the course of negotiating a price. I've learned, by observation, that this gesture signifies he's reached his breaking point, and I can go no further in pushing for a lower price. When he's gone as far as he can go in giving me the best price on a specific product, he'll precede that point in the negotiation process by pausing, taking off his glasses, and raising his tongue to touch the top of his lip.

When this happens, I know that I've received the best deal I can get from him.

And, in turn, when I'm on the giving end of a negotiation with him, I employ the same non-verbal gestures and direct them back to him. If he asks for a price increase that I can not agree to, I pause and put my hand to my forehead – I do not wear glasses, so I can't mirror that gesture – and place my tongue outside my mouth and onto the top of my lip.

Amazingly, when I go through this routine, this vendor backs off. He recognizes, from my non-verbal replay, that I can not accept what he's offering.

This is not a simple game of monkey-see-monkey-do that's played by children. It is, rather, a far more sophisticated and subtle technique of appealing to the subconscious preferences of your opponent.

If you're sitting across a desk from someone with whom you're negotiating, and you are desperately trying to build rapport, try this non-verbal mirroring. If they've crossed their legs, soon afterward, cross yours. If they fold their arms while talking, at some point, fold yours after you begin to speak. When they lean inward to make a point, do the same when you have something important to say. Before long, you'll find that your subject will be following your lead in marking-out body language in an effort to maintain the rapport you've established with them.

That's right. If you are successful in mirroring your subject and you have been successful in establishing rapport, your subject will now subconsciously follow your lead, in order to maintain the rapport that has been established between the two of you.

Conversely, if you're trying to break rapport or disrupt a perceived advantage that your opponent has taken, you can do this by mis-matching your subject both verbally and non-verbally. If they speak to you visually, answer them kinesthetically. If they fold their arms and stand up straight, position yourself in a relaxed posture with your hands behind your back. If they should sit up straight and speak rather quickly, cross your legs and respond slowly.

You'll find this to be an effective defense mechanism that will break your opponent's ability to gain the upper-hand and advantage on you. It may also frustrate them into becoming more vulnerable to be overwhelmed by you and your technique to be persuasive.

When your opponent says something that is agreeable to you, match them both verbally and non-verbally. When they get off on to an area that you don't find to your liking, begin mis-matching them.

Before long, if rapport has been established, you'll find your subject responding positively to you and your mirroring, and steering clear of areas that will illicit a mis-matching response by you.

This brings us to pacing and leading.

Pacing is the act of changing your behavior in order to match that of your opponent. Like a chameleon changing color in order to match his environment, in pacing, you consciously change your behavior to match your opponent.

You pace your opponent by marking-out their specific style and idiosyncrasies. Once identified, you then begin the quest to match them effectively.

In a horse race, one horse, regardless if it's the favorite or long shot, sets the pace right out of the gate. The other horses must then struggle to maintain the pace the lead horse has set, and must mark the lead horse and change their style of running in order to stay competitive.

Similarly, *you* will pace your opponent. You will mark them and their key words and change your style to stay with them in order to build rapport.

Leading will only occur when rapport has been conclusively established. It is then, and only then, that you'll be able to begin leading your opponent to your own point of view.

You will find that your opponent will begin to move in your direction, both verbally and non-verbally, once a strong rapport has been established. Now they'll follow your lead in order to maintain that established rapport.

For example, let's say you've been successful in establishing rapport, and now you're mirroring your subject physically. Soon, you notice that when you cross your legs, your opponent does the same. You fold your arms, and again, they do the same.

Now, you present a statement, and they follow your lead and agree with you. They're subconsciously trying to maintain the rapport that's been established. They don't want to break it by disagreeing.

Begin this process by first trying to build rapport. Next, start to mirror your subject both verbally and non-verbally. Then, begin pacing by changing your behavior to match your opponent. Finally, you may start to lead your subject to your thoughts and your ideas. You may be surprised how easily they'll follow.

One easy way to begin to build rapport is by complimenting your subject.

"That suit looks terrific on you."

You've not only complimented your subject's taste in clothing, but you've also complimented their looks.

The compliment pleases your opponent's ego and it also favorably influences their opinion of you. You've begun to build rapport quickly, and soon you'll be off to the races.

Now you can begin the process of mirroring, pacing, and, finally, leading.

Leading will work for you only after you've established significant rapport with your subject. That person will follow your lead and struggle to maintain your pace rather than risk breaking or losing that very pleasing and desirable rapport that has been established.

LESSON TWELVE

Positive thinking

There could literally be volumes of words written about positive thinking and the power behind it.

One of the best selling books on this subject was written by Dr. Norman Vincent Peale, and is titled, *The Power of Positive Thinking.*

Peale has drawn extensive theories from the premise that positive thinking is a valuable and very powerful force. In his writing, however, Peale has intertwined the power of prayer so closely to the power of positive thinking that he presented them as a nexus dependent upon each other.

While I wouldn't venture to underestimate the power of spirituality or prayer, I'm not sure that the two are dependent or connected any more so than the power of prayer is connected to say, good hygiene. One may draw positive energy from prayer, but prayer need not to first exist in order to create positive thinking in the human species.

However, in *The Power of Positive Thinking*, Dr. Peale convincingly describes the power and energy derived from positive thinking.

Peale is very convincing in his premise that positive thinking will provide you with a distinct advantage over those who do not seek to access this power source. The advantage gained is similar to the edge achieved by employing the techniques of subliminal appeal.

Positive thinking generates a strong sense of confidence to those who use it. Confidence will produce positive results more often than not. Positive thinkers are winners. Whereas, you will often find negative thinkers to be losers.

This may sound to be an over-simplification. But you'll find it to be true time and time again. It is virtually amazing how many negative or bad things happen to people who think negatively.

Simply put, negative thinkers inflict more pain and suffering on themselves than they do their environment. They rarely realize their own potential. The biggest tool to use in overcoming them is to continue to employ positive thinking when confronting them. This positive thinking will confuse and confound them because it is foreign to their thought processes.

If you expect to lose any contest or debate you undertake, you are sure to increase your chances of doing so by thinking that way.

It is important to eliminate any negative or foul thoughts you would have about yourself or your ability.

Stop, pause, and imagine those negative thoughts to be the flame burning on top of an imaginary candle that is directly in front of you. Focus on the candle and the flame and then, inhale. Hold that breath. Exhale. As you expel the air and blow out, direct it at the imaginary candle. Extinguish that flame before you, and as you do, imagine that you have also extinguished any negative thoughts you have about yourself, your ability, or your situation.

Proceed now with a renewed confidence, one that previously did not exist in your mind. This newfound confidence has given you a positive perspective about yourself, your ability, and the situation at hand. Now, you are free to meet your task with an enthusiasm that you could not even imagine if you were to have maintained your previous negative attitude.

I always thought that during all the verbal sparring and spirited exchanges that occur between two fighters before a prizefight in boxing, that one of the fighters truly believes that he is the better and stronger fighter of the two. The other boxer, whoever he may be, I imagine to be a self-doubter. No matter what he may say for public consumption, deep-down inside of him he would hear this little voice telling him, "I really can't keep up with this guy, he's better than me." Those self-doubts keep rising to the top of his mind no matter how hard he may try to repress them.

I doubt that anyone has documented information of studies which examine the relationship between positive thinking and the outcome of prizefights. However, I would venture to guess that the truly confident thinking fighter beats the negative thinking guy in the majority of the contests.

I'd, also, be willing to bet that those negative thinking boxers get their clocks cleaned in the ring on a regular basis.

Positive thinking begets confidence. As confidence grows, so does your ability to succeed. As you succeed, the degree of positive thinking and confidence you exude begins to grow stronger. It may begin small, but it grows with a snowballing effect. As this snowball grows, it becomes a rather formidable force for your opponent to face.

Expect to do well, and you will succeed.

Expect good things to happen, and they often do.

Expect to win, and you will.

There are those, as the saying goes, who see the glass as being half-empty. Others, it is said, see the glass as half-full.

Visualize yourself as a winner, who sees the glass full, and you will train your mind to think and work positively.

The energy that is generated by your positive thinking will emanate from within you and project to those around you. You will find that people will be attracted to this positive energy and drawn to it like moths to a bright light.

There is a certain vibration created by the power your positive thinking has produced. The people around you will find that vibration to be magnetic. Conversely, that same vibration will both shake and rattle your opposition.

The genuine confidence that you possess will not go unnoticed by your foes. They will be forced to deal with it, regardless of how intimidated they may be by it.

Earlier, it was recommended to be coy and to keep your cards close to your vest. Don't be shy, however, about the power and energy transmitted by your positive thinking – allow it to shine through. It has presented you with a comfortable confidence that has also been noticed by your opposition. However, do not allow your energy to be your own undoing by becoming or acting overconfident.

Overconfidence is rooted in ignorance. Do not fall prey to it.

Just as you want to avoid being overconfident, also, do not allow your confidence to be perceived as arrogance by those around you. You want your confident aura to be engaging to those near you, not repulsive.

There is a fine line between the reverence of Sunday morning and the reverie of Saturday night. That line is equally thin to those who distinguish a confident person from an arrogant one. Be secure, but not cocksure. Demonstrate an easy and insouciant manner in your presentations. Avoid being condescending. Be confident and assured, and most importantly, be yourself.

Think strong, be strong.

Think good, be good.

Think positive, be positive.

Positive thinkers are winners.

Be one.

LESSON THIRTEEN

Gestures

A smile is as powerful as it is simple. It may be the world's most universally recognized gesture. From country to country, continent to continent, and from birth to death, it is and expression of goodness and contentment.

Also, it is very easy to send or give to another. It requires almost no effort and it costs you nothing.

For all the ease and goodness of it, you'd think that everyone be using it much more than they do.

Early on, I was inspired by a proverb, which was featured on the back of a Beach Boys' album cover, that was attributed to Indian Wisdom: *"The smile you send out returns to you."*

Think about that, and realize how wise and true that proverb actually is.

In high school, I had a teacher who was especially frugal. In seeking his advise about the difficulties I may have been having at school, or with life as a teenager in general, he told me to keep smiling and be as pleasant as I could be to as many people as possible.

"It doesn't cost you anything to smile or to be nice," he would say. Coming from him, the cost was important. In his experience, he had discovered an exceptional value for his money – the power of a smile. His words though, have stuck with me. I think of them often.

I remember a situation regarding a girl I knew in high school. She wasn't very popular, a bit heavy, and not too attractive. She would walk through the school hallways without any friends by her side and a dour expression on her sullen face.

Acting on the advice of my teacher, I would give her a friendly smile whenever I passed her. It did not take much effort on my part and I had no ulterior motive. I was extending her much more courtesy than most others were willing to show her.

At one point during that year, trouble loomed for me in a certain classroom when I was called upon to describe an assignment to the class. I was unprepared and looked directly into the stern expression of a soon-to-be-angry teacher.

Although I never asked, this unpopular and mostly unrecognized girl didn't hesitate. Before I even knew it, she'd slipped me her assignment paper for me to present as my own.

At that moment, the smile that I had been sending out to her was returned to me. It was a lesson learned. Send out those smiles. They do good for you and for those that you send them to, as well. Plus, they often do, indeed, come back to you.

Smiles illicit strong and positive feelings and responses from those people who receive them, especially those who are identified as visual people.

A smile is an excellent gesture to use as an *anchor* on people who are the visual type. An anchor is a word or a gesture that you would use to establish positive feelings in a conversational situation with the person with whom you are conversing. Once you've anchored positive feelings with your word or gesture, you would repeat that same word or gesture in a later part of the conversation when you want to recreate positive feelings.

For example, let's say your wife, who happens to be a visual person, wants to go out to dinner. She gets herself all dressed-up and ready to go. When you see her, you tell her she looks "really nice" and you smile. The words and the smile illicit strong positive feelings in her. You have anchored those good feelings visually with a smile.

The problem you are now facing is, your wife wants to go to some fancy French restaurant, and you were hoping to go to a steak restaurant.

After some debate you say, "Honey, I was really looking forward to sharing a 'really nice' steak dinner with you tonight." Immediately after the statement, you smile, just as you did when you told her how good she looked earlier.

You have retrieved the anchor, which you had previously set in positive feelings. The words, "really nice" and the smile, which anchored good feelings in her, were recalled to recapture those good feelings and associate them with your new idea.

It really isn't playing fair, and she really doesn't stand a chance. But, guess what? It works – she agrees with you. You win, and it's steaks for everyone.

Although the smile is perhaps the easiest gesture and the best choice of an anchor to use on visual people, other gestures and words may also be used as anchors.

In my daytime job, I run a chain of retail bedding stores. I sometimes get the chance to work on the sales floor and deal directly with customers.

I remember an instance when a customer, who I identified to be an auditory, came in and gave me his own anchor to use directly back on him. I actually stole his anchor in anticipation of using it back on him. This "stealing" of anchors is good usage of the technique of anchoring, because it virtually guarantees that the anchor, which you will be using, is going to be pleasing to the person on whom you are using it. It is an extension of the mirroring and imaging that was discussed in Lesson Eleven.

The customer explained to me that he was experiencing back pain and his doctor recommended that he invest in a new mattress set. This customer explained that he had a curved spine and that his doctor recommended that a new and firm bed would help straighten his spine and allow him to feel better. As he said this, he snapped his fingers and ran his hand through an imaginary straight line before him.

I recognized the finger snap and the hand motion to be his anchor.

I presented a few mattress sets to him. When I got to the mattress I wanted him to buy, I described it by relating a story to it. Remember, auditories like stories.

I told him the true story of a customer who had recently come in to the store and was also suffering the ill-effects of a bad back. This particular customer was in so much back pain that it was difficult for her to stand up straight without feeling some discomfort. That customer, I told the man, had selected this particular mattress. After sleeping on it for just one week, the customer had returned to the store to say that, she'd already enjoyed considerable back relief from the new mattress. I recounted how the customer described the improved condition of her back, and how she told me of her ability to stand straight without the back pain she had previously experienced.

As I relayed the story of how this new mattress had improved the customer's back condition and had helped to straighten her slouching posture, I snapped my fingers and ran my hand through an imaginary straight line before me.

I retrieved the anchor.

And yes, he bought it, and the mattress set, too.

Gestures that have to do with touch or feel are good anchors to use on kinesthetics.

A pat on the back, a touch on the shoulder, or a grab of the arm can all be successful anchors to use on kinesthetics. Using them in a similar fashion as described above will help them to work for you.

Establish a good feeling and anchor it with a word or gesture. Then, make your pitch and retrieve the anchor that you earlier associated with a positive feeling.

Remember, even when working with auditories and kinesthetics, the use of a smile can be very powerful for you. Those smiles need not be only directed to visuals for them to be effective. Because of their positive nature and the good feelings that are universally associated with them, smiles can be used on all home-base type of people.

They work, and you will find that those you do send out often return to you.

Keep sending them.

LESSON FOURTEEN

Morning people

To me, one of the great mysteries of life are those who people who claim that they aren't morning people.

There are those who can rise and shine with the break of dawn, and there are those who can't. Or so they say.

I am not sure what this, "I am not a morning person," means. But, it sounds like an excuse explaining why they don't function well in the AM hours.

As I see it, if you have to wake-up in the AM, you'd better be a morning person. Should you have the misfortune of not awakening from your sleep, then you're definitely not a morning person – at least not on that particular day.

If you are blessed to wake-up, you are, or you had better fast become, a morning person. On any given day, there are many people on this planet who definitely *are not* morning people. In fact, they will not be afternoon, evening, or even night people, for that matter, ever again. It's all over for them – they're dead!

Reconsider the claim, "I am not a morning person," and recognize how ludicrous of a statement it is.

Waking up and claiming not to be a morning person would be like becoming hungry and exclaiming, "I am not an eating person."

It just doesn't make any sense.

If I really thought that I had some deficiency in the morning hours that put me at a disadvantage with the rest of the world, I don't think I'd be too willing to share that inadequacy with anyone else. I'd be embarrassed by my personal failure, and I'd be working hard to correct it.

Yet, these self-described "non-morning people" are very quick, if not anxious, to inform those around them of their self-diagnosed malady.

If you are one of those people, who have used this "I am not a morning person" excuse, work to establish patterns in your life that will allow you to become a morning person. If you feel your physiology is not capable of functioning efficiently in the AM hours, no matter how hard you try, begin waking up one or two hours before the rest of the civilized world and spend this time by yourself doing routine or mundane activities. Make coffee, read the paper, or clean up around the house. Give yourself time to assimilate into the fabric of the day.

Now, when the rest of the world is waking up to their morning, it's past that time for you – you're now in mid-morning. You don't have to be at a disadvantage meeting and dealing with all those happy morning people, who are all so bright and cheerful, from a handicapped position. It's almost afternoon to you!

However, should you find yourself needing to wake up three, four, or five hours earlier than normal to work this strategy, it's time to rethink this position and find a new plan of attack.

If you are ever associated with people who make the morning claim, and actually believe it to be true, take the initiative.

Confront, debate, and conduct as many negotiations as possible with them in the morning hours. It's when they're the most vulnerable.

For no other reason other than the preconceived notion they have about themselves, these non-morning people will go about their AM business somewhat tentatively, expecting to fail.

Schedule negotiations with these people as early as possible, and arrange the meetings to take place at the location of your choice. You will be confronting a person who is not operating at peak performance at a location that adds an additional degree of discomfort. Now, you will not only be enjoying a distinct energy advantage, but you also will have the benefit of the home-field advantage.

It is really quite a shame that there are people out there who are willing to write-off such an important and beautiful part of the day. Many good things happen to those who start their day early.

Why?

Well, for one thing, you are not competing against a full complement of people out there in the work force. Many of your competitors are sleep-walking through their morning routines. The deck is definitely stacked in your favor.

As I mentioned earlier, I work in a retail store. I can recall numerous occasions when the phone rang, well in advance of the store's opening, with a customer on the other end wanting to place an order. When this happens, I often wonder if a competing company had lost the business because this customer may have tried there first, only to have the call go unanswered. It is a good case of the early bird catching the worm, and in my case, getting the order.

Another benefit of being an early riser is that by beginning the day's events early, you have a greater period of time to correct, or make right, anything that hasn't gone well the first time around on that day.

Often, as you know, events do not always proceed as planned. When you begin early, you have a larger window of opportunity to explore corrections. If you have a project with a specific deadline, the earlier you begin, the more time you will have to complete your work. By starting early, you allow yourself the luxury of working at a relaxed and comfortable pace, permitting you to complete your assignment in an unhurried and, perhaps, more accurate fashion.

I think back to my college days when, for whatever the reason, many students would wait until the last minute to complete an assignment. They would be forced to pull, what we'd call an all-nigher, to complete their work. More often than not, the all-nighers would produce an sub-par effort and an ultimately inferior product.

Adding insult to injury, these students would then have to suffer the ill effects of the physical fall-out that came along with missing the benefit of a healthy night of sleep, thus rendering them definite non-morning person status for the next day, or even two.

I once heard the famous college and pro football player, Paul Hornung, joke on an NFL broadcast that his daddy used to tell him to get married in the morning. That way, he said, if things didn't work out, he hadn't ruined the whole day.

Start your day early. Enjoy the beauty of the morning and benefit of your early effort throughout the balance of the day. You'll find it gives you an advantage that many others are willing to relinquish, and in some cases, forego entirely.

Be a morning person simply by making the morning an operational and productive part of your day.

LESSON FIFTEEN

Give me your tired

Just as you would like to confront those non-morning people during AM hours, there is another group of individuals who will offer you an equally large advantage. It's those sleep-deprived people who go around constantly complaining about being tired or groggy from a lack of healthy sleep. Many of these people go about their day's business in a dazed funk.

Both the body and the mind require a specific amount of rest and sleep to recharge and nourish themselves. Many overlook the need to sleep and, consequently, it reduces their mental sharpness and often renders them irritable.

Dr. Mark Mahowald, of the Minnesota Regional Sleep Disorders Center in Minneapolis, suggests that many people downplay the importance of sleep.

"Many believe that sleep loss has no consequences," says Dr. Mahowald. "In short, this is untrue...sleep is not a negotiable need," he says.

Without a healthy night of sleep, many people go day-to-day with a lack of energy and productivity, causing them to operate significantly below their personal level of peak performance.

These people are suffering from what Dr. William Dement, Director of Stanford University's Sleep Disorders Clinic and Research Center in Palo Alto, California, has defined as *sleep deprivation*.

A significant number of people are operating at only a fraction of their capability because of this sleep deprivation, which some doctors are referring to as a sleep debt.

Research being done at Stanford indicates that many adults today are in debt up to their eyelids over this loss of sleep.

Research shows that even one sleepless night undermines creativity and coping skills. The day after a sleepless night, most people are less spontaneous, flexible, and capable of original thought. If they concentrate hard enough, they can perform routine tasks – unless they lose a second night's sleep. Then, even the performance of mundane chores suffers.

These daytime sleep walkers are easy to spot by their appearance. And, like the non-morning people, they are quite eager to share the plight of their drowsiness with you. They will almost always tell you how tired they are.

They are especially easy targets. Winning them over, while no great accomplishment, is a victory, just the same, in a negotiating situation.

However, be sure that you are to maintain your advantage by staying fresh, well-rested, and prepared before any scheduled negotiations.

Make sleep and staying well-rested a priority and it will impact your life in a positive manner. Your mind needs to be sharp and limber for you to exploit an advantage over the tired people of the world.

Most others are either ignorant to the importance of good, healthy sleep or have simply chosen to ignore the fact. When competing against these people, your well-rested mind and body will provide you with an edge in energy and sharpness that the weary will be unable to match.

LESSON SIXTEEN

Contrarians

Those people who continually have ideas and view points that are in conflict with the views and ideas that are presented to them by others, are the group that we will refer to as the contrarians.

It may be that these people feel a need to not be in conformity with what is usual or expected. Or, perhaps, they enjoy the role of devil's advocate, operating as the person who champions the less accepted or approved cause, merely for the sake of argument.

It is also possible, that these people are not very secure about themselves. They may have a need to strike out and create a discordant situation by not agreeing with, or accepting, the terms of any point-of-view that is placed to them for approval. They may feel the need to set their own stage; and their ego will not allow them to perform on one that has been predetermined.

Or, maybe, these people are simply the argumentative type who are contrary by nature to most thoughts and ideas that are presented to them.

These contrarians would be good people to take along when you go out to buy a car – they'd be sure to find a reason not to buy it, and they'd surely get the dealer to drop the price. But, in general communication situations, they can be difficult, if not impossible, to deal with.

You may find it difficult to understand the reason why they need to create conflict. But, it is less important that you understand their reasoning than it is that you develop a strategy in coping with them.

There are some people who, for whatever reason, are not going to agree with you or your ideas. There is little, if anything, that you can do to change that.

Instead of trying to overwhelm these people with your argument of reason, it is probably a better spent effort to employ a damage control strategy and minimize the issues of conflict you will have with them.

In these confrontational situations, there will probably be many issues of conflict at hand between you and your opponent. Yield on those issues that are either unimportant or less important to you. It is critical, however, that your opponent perceives a sense of victory in this exchange.

It is equally critical that you do not capitulate on the issues that are important to you. You must stand firm and continue to express you views in a calm but sure manner. The fact that you have already surrendered on some issues sends your opponent a clear message that you are not excessively obstinate to the point of being totally unyielding. You've already made some concessions, so you have every right to stand firm, by common reasoning, on issues of which you have strong or passionate views.

However, remember you're dealing with a contrarian here. Just about anything you say will be challenged. So be prepared for the impending stuggle.

These contrarians are usually easy to spot. Like a pushy salesman who tries to close the sale too early and too often, the contrarians will disagree in a similar fashion. It won't be long into a conversation or discussion that you will realize just what you're up against. These contrarians will show their colors quickly.

When trying to build rapport with a contrarian, lay back, listen, and resist expressing your ideas and viewpoints early in the exchange. Instead, allow the contrarian to express their views on the subject matter.

When the contrarian presents their views, you are now in the position to agree and reinforce the contrarian's opinions and, consequently, establish rapport.

The contrarian will find your support of their ideas agreeable. With the reinforcement of their views, rapport will quickly follow.

At this point of the exchange, you'll be in a better position to lead the contrarian to your own point of view. Now, with rapport high, the contrarian will struggle to maintain rapport with you because, on the surface, it appears that you share their position.

Another strategy that can be used on the contrarian is the old-fashioned, Huck Finn, reverse psychology.

Once you've recognized the contrarian before you to be an especially active and ornery one, you can lead them to your point of view simply by presenting the exact opposite view, to the viewpoint you actually hold, merely for the contrarian's public consumption.

The contrarian, of course, will debate your point. You, in a magnanimous gesture, can acquiesce to the contrarian and their argument.

However, your apparent compromise is, in actuality, not a compromise at all. You actually compromised back to your original idea.

For example, say you want to take your vacation after the Fourth of July. Your boss, who is a definite contrarian, will most likely take exception to that for reasons that only he knows. He'll probably present you with a litany of reasons why that vacation time will not be acceptable.

With that knowledge, you confront your boss and tell him that you would like to schedule your vacation. You tell him that you think it would be better if you took your vacation *before* the Fourth of July, because that date precedes the company's busy season.

Being the contrarian that he is, your boss, of course, disagrees. He tells you that going on vacation before the company's busy season will leave you short on preparation and planning. He tells you that he thinks you will be needed to be in the office before the Fourth of July. Instead, he suggests that you vacation *after* the Fourth.

Point, match, and game. You win!

It may sound simple, it may sound condescending, and it may even sound foolish. But, rest assured, this strategy does work and the contrarian never sees it coming.

Once you've made your point and won the debate, hightail out of there and away from the contrarian. Any further dialogue with the contrarian can only result in an upset of your previously earned victory. And, most importantly, don't gloat over your victory – at least until you are out-of-sight of the contrarian. After that, you can howl like the wind with self-gratifying laughter.

LESSON SEVENTEEN

Trying to reason with the hurricane season

Sometimes, there is no degree of eloquence or persusiveness that can change or influence the course of certain events.

There are some cases that you can not prevent from happening. And, there are other issues which you can do nothing to change. Simply put, there are some things that are just out of your control.

The title of this chapter shares the honor with that of a Jimmy Buffett song, and it may focuses on how futile some attempts to effect change can be.

In Buffett's *Trying To Reason With The Hurricane Season*, the solution to his particular dilemma was to stumble next door to the bar and have a Bloody Mary. The theme of that song is Buffett's lament concerning his realization that there is little he could do, other than cope, with the impending hurricane season.

Similarly, there is nothing that can be done about many instances in life, concerning both acts of God *and* the acts of people. Some things are going to happen regardless of anyone's input, including your own. You just can't change certain events from happening.

In obvious instances, it's rather clear that you could not prevent a hurricane from occuring. And equally so, you can't change the behavior of some people at certain times. It is in those instances that no degree of study, strategy, or manipulation will change the action about to take place.

When you realize that you are in this type of situation, take a step back, get quiet, and observe what is happening around you.

If you assess a situation to be one in which you can't emerge a winner, don't allow it to bother you. Do not expend any energy, or worry, on this subject. Go on. Any continued attention to this issue will only prevent you from focusing on issues and events that you can influence. Instead of fretting over these issues, make appropriate plans to accommodate the results of these unchangeable events that take place.

I would imagine that those people who spend their time fretting about an impending hurricane are far less prepared for it than those who have readied themselves and buttressed their homes against it and its fury. Those who recognize that there is nothing they can do to prevent it, but also realize that there is plenty that they can do to prevent or minimize its damage, are obviously the far wiser.

It's the difference between responding and reacting to a situation. Now, you may ask yourself, "What's the difference between responding or reacting to something?"

Plenty.

A response to a particular situation is a positive occurrence and, it usually will elicit a positive result. Let's say you go to the doctor for an ailment and he gives you treatment for your malady. If you respond to the treatment, you're doing good. You want to hear that you are responding well to what the doctor has prescribed. That's a good sign.

Now, let's take the same example. You go to the doctor for an ailment, but this time, instead of responding, you react to the treatment. That usually means something negative has occurred. Instead of responding to the doctor's treatment, you reacted to it. That's usually not a good sign. A reaction to the treatment means that something has gone wrong.

It's the same in life situations, when you respond in an exchange, it's a good sign. You have responded appropriately to the situation at hand. However, if you react to a life situation, it usually means that you have acted inappropriately, perhaps on emotion and irrational judgment.

Think about those people we spoke of who were awaiting the hurricane. Those who prepared themselves, their families, and their homes for the impending damage are the ones who responded. Whereas, those who, instead of preparing for the damage, ran around wailing, crying, and fretting about what was being forecasted, are the people who reacted to the situation.

Who would you rather be?

There aren't too many people running around trying to reason with hurricane seasons, but it's also apparent that there are some who seem better prepared for them than others. Be prepared and respond to life situations. Try not to react in a negative manner.

When you realize that you're in a no-win situation, take appropriate measures to minimize the degree of damage that will affect you. There are times when your best move will be to take your ball and go home. Any further effort will only compound your losses.

The other issue at hand is, do not overly concern yourself about things of which you have no control. Instead, redirect your energy to issues that you can influence. Any effort on those out-of-your-hands issues will be made in vain. Minimize your anguish and absolve yourself from the worry that accompanies those issues.

I've always been amazed by the insouciance many Southern Californians seem to display about the impending earthquakes that loom on their horizon. These Californians are quite aware that the shaky ground beneath their feet is situated on a very active fault line. Earthquakes and earthshakes are frequent occurrences there. Most scientists and seismologists agree that sometime during the next century a major earthquake of tremendous proportion will occur in that region. The lives of the people living there will be significantly altered, if not gravely threatened.

Still, the overwhelming majority of the people who live in Southern California go about their lives untroubled and unconcerned about the impending doom that has been forecasted to befall them.

Why?

They recognize that there is nothing they can do to prevent this event from happening. They do, in most cases, however, prepare for this disaster by stocking fresh, bottled water, and additional canned food supplies should an earthquake disrupt their water supply or impede their mobility. They have spent their energy on preparedness, and have chosen not to fret over something that they can't control.

Those Californians who don't share their neighbor's nonchalance about the shaky ground upon which they live, in many cases do something about it – they move.

The others who continue to live there have made a decision not to worry about something they can't control. Those people recognize that their worry will not stop the earth from moving. Therefore, they choose not to concern themselves with this impending problem.

Leave it to Californians to be on the cutting-edge of ambivalence.

There is a lesson to be learned here. Don't burden yourself and your mind with issues that are out of the realm of your control. You have nothing to gain from those worries – except ulcers.

Instead, focus you attention on matters where you can make a difference.

And then, make that difference benefit you.

LESSON EIGHTEEN

Don't let it shake you, kid

At one time or another, you've probably been called everything from stupid to pompous. You, like most people, are neither of the two. Instead, you're probably somewhere in-between.

Such is life, and those who choose to live it must carry on in spite of their accusers.

There are always people out there who are ready, if not anxious, to throw stones at a visible target. Their motivation, in many cases, is petty jealously. For whatever reason, they feel threatened by you and the successful image you project to them. They can't compete with that image, so they have no other choice but to knock it down. It is their own insecurities, and lack of self-confidence, that fuels their drive to be negative.

Several years ago, when my wife and I moved into the community where we live, I used to joke that we were perhaps the least recognized people in town. We had complete anonymity – nobody knew us.

But the two children growing up in our house had a way of putting us in touch with our neighbors and the other people in our community.

Before long, my wife and I were associated with many volunteer organizations that involved the children. For several years, my wife was the President of the local PTA, and I was a Commissioner on the Board of Directors for the youth-sports organizations in town.

We derived an enormous amount of satisfaction from working for the benefit of the children in this volunteer work. And, as anyone who has ever been involved in such organizations may know, there is the unfortunate flip-side of dealing with some of the parents. Some are very focused with their own personal agenda and that of their own children. They do not allow themselves to see the whole picture.

For us, however, the overall experience has been a good one, and the great majority of people do indeed respect you and the work you do for these volunteer groups. Still, there are always a few who seem eager to strike out at you, for the reasons that only they know.

After living in the same town for over ten years, my wife and I no longer live in the peaceful anonymity we once enjoyed. Because of the visible position we have been in, more people, now, know us and recognize our faces. While I would like to think we have made many new friends due to our involvement, I'd be naive if I didn't recognize that we've collected a few enemies along the way.

I recently joked to my wife that, now, when we go to any event in our town, at least three of the people there hate us. She insists that I'm exaggerating, but it's not too far from the truth. The reasons for their animosity are petty and self-centered, but they do exist, just the same.

I was recently at a fund-raiser where I met an older gentleman who, in his younger days, had volunteered much of his free time to youth sports. Coincidentally, his wife was also involved with the PTA. We spoke at length about the rewards of giving something back to the community by way of the children who live there. I confided to him that I was disappointed and upset by the people who didn't recognize the good we were doing. I told him of people who consider me more of a devil than a saint due to my involvement.

Maybe it was because he was so distinguished, so well-spoken, and so much older than me, but I found his reply to contain one of the most profound statements ever spoken to me. "Don't let it shake you, kid," he said.

I have, since, taken his words to heart.

As was mentioned in Lesson Twelve, there are winners and losers in this world. Those people, who have the time and desire to knock down others, are the losers. They are threatened by what they see you to be. Your life and your actions are viewed as too complex for them to understand. Consequently, they attack that picture that they see, but do not necessarily understand.

These people often do not see the big picture of situations, but rather they get a myopic glimpse of life through their own tiny, microscope-eyes. Their views are often one dimensional. They see black and white solutions to the Technicolor problems of life. Their sense and awareness of the total picture is far less defined and developed than is that of those they attack. They often have difficulty keeping pace with the people who are their targets.

If you find yourself the target of one of these people, that alone may confirm the fact that you are a winner.

Go on undisturbed by their petty criticism. Any adjustment you make to your behavior, which is based on their input, will only impede your ability to do good and succeed.

Hearken back to your ability to think positive and enjoy the energy and the power you will derive from this asset.

Be confident and be secure.

Those who do the knocking are far less secure than those they feel the need to knock. They know it, and it is why they direct their criticism at you. They hope their criticism will bring you down to their level.

Don't let it shake you, kid. Stay the course and be yourself.

LESSON NINETEEN

Lieutenant Colombo

Another negotiation strategy of which you should be aware, and ultimately prepared to face, is what I call the Lieutenant Colombo approach. Much like Lieutenant Colombo, the Peter Falk character in the famous TV show, there are those who will patronize and dupe you into believing that they are disorganized and unprepared. They attempt to lull you into a sense of false security in your dealings with them. They come on as self-effacing and unpretentious sorts who do not know much, if anything, about the subject at hand.

Should you fall for their trap, you'll soon find out how wrong you were about them. Before you can say, "A wolf in sheep's clothing," you'll have been stung by the Lieutenant Colombo approach.

Being in the furniture business, I have occasion to visit the semi-annual Furniture Market, which is held in High Point, North Carolina. Many of the manufacturers and vendors who are involved in the market are local types who have been born and raised in the local foothills surrounding the market area.

Some come across as good old country types, whose idea of good fashion is not to have any horse "do" sticking to their shoes. However, I've seen many a fancy "New York Suit Type" have his lunch eaten by one of these hayseeds, and not realize it until it was too late. Those country boys don't cotton much to being taken for fools. They often extract revenge by winning in the exchanges that take place with their Yankee counterparts. They may look like jellyfish, but their bite bears a closer resemblance to that of a shark.

The best way to avoid becoming the bait that these sharks eat is to be careful at initial meetings and *never* underestimate the competition.

Some of the world's most rumpled-looking human beings are actually brilliant people. Many of these people are intelligent, but they're too caught up in their own thoughts to concern themselves with something that they view as mundane – that being their own physical appearance.

Others are aware of what their disheveled appearance projects, and they consciously present this dysfunctional image in order to exploit that image to their advantage.

Be careful not to fall prey to either of these types.

Assume that Albert Einstein was alive today, and he was at the next business meeting you were attending. You'd probably dismiss him as a crazy man on the basis of his appearance.

Think about what a shame it would be for you to have missed the opportunity to have met and conversed with one the greatest minds of all-time, all because you prejudged him not to be worth the effort, merely on the basis of his appearance.

Be careful. There are people, who consciously downplay their appearance so that their ability will be underestimated by those around them. Some of these people are outright con-artists. They exploit the advantage afforded them by those who have prejudged them.

In addition to gaining an advantage through their appearance, many will seek to gain a similar advantage by feigning ignorance either at the issue at hand, or of that in general.

Don't be fooled and do not allow yourself to be duped by these people. Stay alert and do not underestimate them.

Many victims have had victories snatched right from their hands when, at the moment of decision, the real Lieutenant Colombo reared his ugly head from the same body that only moments before appeared so safe, sorry, and even pitiful.

Resist judging your opponents until you've concluded all business with them.

There have been countless hot-shots, who have strode confidently into pool halls, only to have been hustled by the most unlikely of candidates, who eventually beat them of their pride and their money.

When confronted by an apparent Lieutenant Colombo approach, begin to mirror your subject. You will stifle any attempt made to gain the upper-hand through this strategy. Your refusal to underestimate and fall prey to their pitch will frustrate any attempt they make to gain an advantage.

Play the equally naïve and unattached approach back to them. They'll be forced to shift gears and switch to a new strategy. Once this is accomplished, you must recognize that you've forced a compromise.

Now, you've gained a double advantage. One, you've smoked-out a potential snake. And two, by forcing your opponent to make the first compromise, you've significantly increased your chances of gaining yet another compromise.

After this reversal, you may have your opponent on the ropes. Go for the kill before they have the opportunity to regroup and regain control of the conversation and the situation.

Try to establish control. Do this by asking questions. You are on the offensive and you now have your opponent on the defensive. Begin to collect information about your opponent and where they seem to be heading with this negotiation. The more information you receive, the better you will have placed yourself to develop a strategy of attack.

If this can be accomplished, extricate yourself from the situation. End the conversation and any impending negotiations concerned.

Merely by not losing to the Lieutenant Colombo at hand, you may have earned a victory.

LESSON TWENTY

Throw yourself at the mercy of the court

There are times when you may have made a rather dramatic stand on a specific issue. Perhaps you've staked your reputation, not to mention a considerable portion of your ego, on a particular issue or endeavor. You have a great deal riding on an issue that you have publicly professed to be yours.

In spite of this, time has proven your dramatic stand to be, euphemistically put, on shaky ground.

In blunt terms, you were dead wrong.

What are your options?

Well, for one thing, you could punt and try again. Another option would be to try to massage reality into the framework of your original idea. That may be difficult, if not impossible, in many instances.

You could try to talk, finesse, or even bullshit your way to a position of safety. Or, you could opt for the simplest and most humble of solutions – admit that you were wrong.

As hard as it may be, admitting the error of your ways can be a very valuable negotiating tool.

A genuine act of contrition in the hands of even the biggest scoundrel has served forgiveness on the plate of some of the world's greatest sinners.

Throughout Biblical stories, for instance, the good Lord has always been quick to dole out absolution, even to the most prolific of sinners. In fact, in many of those stories, he seemed to be somewhat of a sucker. It seemed that any sinner, no matter what his crime, would be granted mercy merely by admitting their guilt, and then asking to be forgiven.

The act of forgiveness is not exclusive to divine powers. Throughout history, those who have done wrong, and then admitted such, have been forgiven both on small and grand-scale misdeeds.

Richard M. Nixon, who in 1973 had to resign from the world's most powerful and prestigious position in disgrace, is a good example. For years, Nixon was ostracized by the American public after his resignation. He became a political pariah who was brandished a disgrace by friend and foe alike. It was only after Nixon did admit to some degree of guilt in the infamous Watergate case that he was able to rise from the ashes of his personal tragedy to become a respected, if not revered, elder statesman during the years before his death.

The saying. "Time heals all wounds," is true. But the healing occurs much more quickly when the injured party is willing to admit culpability for the inflicted wounds.

When you are caught with your pants down, sometimes your best defense isn't to only pull them up.

As mentioned earlier, there will be times when infinite communication skills may not be enough to extract you from a losing situation. While you may have other options to pursue in these cases, the simple admission of guilt, accompanied by your projected remorse, can set you on the road to recovery quicker than any other strategy.

When you are found to be dead wrong, your admission of guilt will stop any continued assault from being heaped upon you and your position. When you've placed yourself in a position of submission, your attackers will cease from any further assault.

What else can an opponent say to, "I'm sorry, I was wrong and you were right?"

There are few aggressive responses that would be an appropriate reply to that humble statement. Even a less-than-gracious opponent would be hard pressed to continue an attack after you have submitted to them and their position.

Being on the receiving end of that submission is easy. The difficult and humbling part is delivering that message. However difficult that may be, it is a critical lesson to be learned, and then employed in communications and negotiations. You have to know when to run, and conversely, when to fight.

As was mentioned in Lesson Seventeen, sometimes your best move is to take your ball and go home.

Similarly, when you find yourself facing a checkmate position, your finest move may be to accept defeat, apologize for your misdeeds, and submit to your opponent and their terms.

You can't win them all. That is a lesson you must eventually embrace.

Growing up on the city streets of South Philadelphia, I learned that lesson at an early age. I guess you could call it street smarts. It doesn't take too many beatings on the street to catch on to the concept rather quickly. You learn when to run. You'd be amazed at how easy that lesson can be drummed into you.

Equally so, life on the city streets affords you a certain confidence to know when to stand your ground and, if necessary, fight.

It's not so different in day-to-day communications.

You, through your education and experience, have established a sense of street smarts. This sense has become a basic instinct to you. You have an innate ability to analyze situations. You know when to stand your ground and fight. The competitor in you kicks into gear automatically when you are challenged. The communication skills you've already developed put you up to the task at hand to do verbal battle.

It's the surrender or submission variable that's more difficult to embrace and employ in those situations and negotiations where it may be needed. You may find this tactic less agreeable to your basic instinct.

However, when the situation calls, you must be able to place better reasoning ahead of your own ego. As difficult as it may be to surrender to your opponent on their terms, sometimes, it may be your best move.

I remember a situation when I, as a teenager, was responsible for cutting a few lawns in the neighborhood where I lived. One property owner had me oversee the mantainence of his entire yard. On one particular occasion, I had been irresponsible and had not attended to the property in question for more than two weeks. I was being seduced by the typical distractions that often capture the attention of a fifteen year-old boy. I remember riding my bike past the unkempt property and feeling a pain in my stomach caused by my own thoughtlessness. Still, I neglected my duties. And while I did this, the grass kept growing higher and higher.

Finally, I could no longer avoid the untidy property or its owner. I had to face them. I went to the house, drew a deep breath, and rang the bell.

"Well, hello young man, what do you have to say for yourself? Our yard is a mess and you have been totally negligent in your schedule of required maintenance. What are you going to do?" asked the very unhappy homeowner.

I don't know where it came from, but I did something that must have come very naturally to me because I did it without a preconceived plan.

I said, "I am very sorry, and I have no excuse for my behavior. I was very wrong to have neglected your property and I am truly sorry for that. I will correct this problem and I promise you it will never happen again."

I still remember my amazement to his response. He accepted my apology and he was *not* going to kill me. I was sorry and he believed me. He did not tar and feather me. In fact, he seemed touched by the sincerity of my apology. He was kind and even understanding of my behavior. I remember him saying, "I know what it's like. I was fifteen at one time, too."

"Wow, it worked," I thought to myself. I should have thought of this before. From that date forward, I never forgot the power of a good act of contrition.

Allow your sense of reason to overcome your ego, and then do the right thing. You'll find yourself in a better position to proceed with further negotiations when you emerge from a surrender position than should you have chosen to pursue an impossible battle to its bloody conclusion.

In street-life situations, those who surrender to the terms at hand are far better prepared to carry and pursue future issues than are those who stayed and fought to the bitter end. It would be acceptable if the end were that of the opponent, but, unfortunately, in most of those impossible situations the bitter end our foolish warrior faces is often his own.

If you've determined after evaluation of the situation that you, in fact, have been proven wrong and cannot win the negotiation at hand you now must decide if you are to navigate a course of surrender, or find a passageway of flight.

If you have determined that you cannot win, and the conditions at hand will not allow you an escape route to reload and try again, your best move may be to surrender and throw yourself at the mercy of the court. Now you must hope for the best and immediately begin to assess the situation so that you may analyze your loss.

At this point, you may immediately begin to position yourself for a future victory based on the information you've gleaned from this loss. This information should help you avoid the same errors that contributed to this most recent defeat.

LESSON TWENTY-ONE

The battle of the sexes

It has been going on since the beginning of time, and will probably continue until the end of eternity. It is the battle of the sexes.

This battle is fought on nearly all fronts. Sex and sex appeal are employed and exploited at almost every turn of our lives.

Turn on the TV, and commercials tell you to do this or buy that so that you'll be more attractive to the opposite sex. At shopping malls, stores direct their appeal to the ego of the sex at which its product is aimed. The goal is to send a message that the product displayed will have a positive effect on the opposite sex if or when purchased.

Psychologists, in fact, have known for years that many advertisements carry subliminal sexual messages that are often received, but rarely recognized, by the audience at which they are directed. The next time you see a magazine ad for an alcoholic beverage, look closely at the flow of the liquid displayed to be coming from the bottle out of which it is being poured. Or, check out the ice cubes sitting in the awaiting glass. Have you ever seen ice cubes that looked like that? There are more images in those doctored photos than one could ever imagine. The advertisers call it subliminal seduction.

Sex. It's a tool that is being used in selling almost everything that is for sale – including you and your ideas. That's right. Sex and sex appeal can have an effect on what you sell, especially when that commodity is you or your ideas.

For example, say a fine, young gentleman goes to a men's clothing store looking for a new suit. He is soon greeted by a stunningly beautiful saleswoman. She has long raven-red hair, bright sparkling eyes, and a tight fitting black dress that reveals an athletic and well-proportioned figure. If that's not enough, she greets the young man with a smile that radiates the room and sends a bit of a shiver up his spine.

Let's be serious. This is not going to be a sales encounter of the ordinary kind.

With his hand on a specific suit, the young man sheepishly tells the saleswoman that he likes the feel of the fabric of the particular suit he is touching. The saleswoman recognizes the inclination of the shopper – that of a kinesthetic – and *hands* him the suit to try on for size.

As he exits the dressing room and approaches the mirror for a fitting, the saleswoman touches him on the arm and flashes a seductive smile as she tells him how good he looks. In case you didn't notice, she just anchored him. Realizing his kinesthetic tendencies, she used the touch and a smile to anchor his good feelings.

The young man looks in the mirror, and he has to admit, he does look good in this suit.

Before he gets too caught up in the euphoria of the moment, reality crashes down on him as he remembers to look at the price tag hanging down from the right sleeve of the jacket. He glances down to see just how much it's going to cost him to look this good. In a split second, he wonders if he's gone mad or maybe temporarily insane to be considering a suit that will cost him more than his monthly mortgage payment.

Now his mind is racing. He has shifted his thinking to how he can slip out of this suit and gracefully exit the store and this embarrassing situation.

It's not that easy, that raven-hair angel – or is it devil – is lurking over his shoulder and she's smiling. She saunters over to his right, looks him over head-to-toe, and pauses. The young man makes eye contact with this beautiful woman who again flashes him a smile as she simultaneously touches him on the arm. She just retrieved the anchor she previously set. She tells him that he looks terrific and that this is the suit for him.

In an instant, the young man is awash in good feelings about himself and the suit. And, somebody is getting themself a new suit on that day.

If one were to say that he or she would be totally undisturbed by the presence of such a salesperson and the subliminal selling skills that were employed in the previous scene, I'd tell him or her that they're full of it!

However, if the salesperson who greeted our young shopper in the store was a sixty-something, cigar breath, fashion victim, sales*man*, instead of Miss Universe, I'm sure that the young fellow would've been out of that suit, and out of that store, faster than you could say Georgio Armani.

Our shopper would probably have had no problem telling that salesman that the suit he tried on needed to have its decimal points altered.

But with a beautiful attendant, a come-hither look, and subliminal selling skills at play, it just isn't that easy.

And it's the same for women. Ladies, imagine yourself trying on a pair of shoes you realize you can't afford when you're being waited on by a drop-dead, good looking Price Charming. It's much harder to say no in a sales situation when you're simultaneously being sold and subliminally seduced.

It makes little difference if the subject is a man or a woman.

There is a magnetic power which emanates from sex and its related appeal. It's something we confront everyday. How well you handle it is what will separate the men from the boys and the woman from the girls.

Master sales trainer, Zig Ziglar, cautions his followers to avoid using sex or sex appeal in their sales presentations. He warns that, while using sex appeal in a sales encounter may make an occasional sale, it won't provide a solid foundation on which to build a successful sales career.

It is wise to avoid using sex as a selling strategy at all. The worst thing that could happen to you is that, after successful application of it as a selling strategy, you fall prey to the allure of calling on it in future selling situations. Before, long, you'll find yourself missing sales, and perhaps even causing trouble for yourself, because of a developed propensity to use sex appeal to sell you and your ideas.

Say for instance, you're presenting your ideas to a man and a woman, who happen to be husband and wife. You are establishing tremendous rapport with the woman, but not with the man. You recognize this and are playing to her attention. The husband also realizes this, and is not only feeling slighted in this exchange, but, in addition, he's becoming angry with the attention you're showering on his wife. He will torpedo any effort you make to attempt to effectively sell yourself or your ideas to the both of them. Worse yet, you may even end up getting slugged.

Guys, even if you are the Robert Redford type, and ladies, even if you are the Madonna type, your charm and sex appeal will eventually fail you in what may be a critical situation.

Avoid becoming unwittingly dependent on your own charm and sex appeal by not calling on it in any selling situation. In addition to the caveats previously mentioned, those who do exploit their charm and sex appeal to their own advantage are often very transparent people. Their moves are often telegraphed to most around them and their motives are easily recognized to be less than honest.

And when you're trying to build rapport and be persuasive, the last thing you want to be perceived as, is less than honest.

You build rapport by building trust and confidence in yourself and your ideas. When you've established this in your audience, you will have increased your ability to be persuasive by dramatic proportions.

Much of the charm of a confident personality is that a secure individual doesn't need to summon their own sex appeal in order to be persuasive. A humble, yet confident, approach will not go unnoticed by your audience.

Once again, be yourself and be confident. Your charm and sex appeal will shine through without a contrived effort to exploit it. Save your charm and sex appeal for romantic encounters.

There's much more to you and your personality. A truly confident person need not resort to sophomoric appeals to the audience's libido in order to be persuasive.

Even in instances where you feel a certain chemistry with your audience or subject, which would seem appropriate for you to call upon your sex appeal to increase your persuasiveness, be careful and proceed cautiously. Even then, refrain from using this angle as the focus of your presentation. As was mentioned earlier, your natural charm and sex appeal will be more alluring and attractive to your audience just by the fact that you don't appear to be ostensibly calling upon it in a selling situation.

If you genuinely possess any charm at all, it will be carried through on the strength of your own personality.

LESSON TWENTY-TWO

Be strong – be good

There is a negotiation technique that is less frequently used and even less frequently recognized. It is the be strong – be good technique.

I learned it while in college, and once I recognized its strength and usefulness, I began to employ it in appropriate situations with favorable results.

During my senior year in college, I remember that many of the students in my department were excited about meeting the Department Chairman of the Business School. We knew that this man had served in a similar capacity at one of the world's most prestigious business colleges. He had been retired, but was lured back to the world of academia by the challenge of taking the top job in the Business Department at Rutgers University.

Upon meeting him for the first time, I remember my disappointment at the image and persona of this miserable and nasty old man who was supposed to lead our department to great, new heights. He was nothing like I had expected or had hoped for him to be. He was gruff and bad-tempered, and he seemed to view the students with contempt rather than respect.

I went home that day crestfallen. I had expected so much more in our new leader.

On my next encounter with him, this crusty old man had been transformed to a vibrant, responsive, and charming personality. I was amazed by this change, but also, I was overwhelmed with pleasure. I remember thinking to myself, "Wow, this guy really is the greatest."

I was not only pleased with his personality change, but more importantly, I was truly appreciative of it.

Afterward, I remember conversing with a fellow student about our new Department Chairman. I told the student of my initial encounter with the new Chairman, and how disappointed I was with his ill-tempered personality. I then relayed how I became enchanted with the dynamic personality I confronted on my very next meeting with him. I remember telling the student how appreciative I was of the Chairman's apparent interest in me and what I wonderful person I now thought him to be.

My fellow student, who was obviously much brighter and better prepared than me, went on to tell me that the mean and ugly demeanor displayed by the professor was deliberate. It was a planned set-up, which he planned to follow with his true personality at a later date. It was actually an orchestrated business tactic used to increase the positive feelings his audience would feel toward him upon his transformation from frog to prince. His theory was, once you've first seen the dark side of a situation, you're then much more likely to appreciate its lighter or positive side.

This man knew what he was doing and where he was going in those future encounters. But he wanted his audience to really appreciate it when he got there. He had to show the students his dark side, if they were to truly appreciate his goodness. It was a total set-up and a blatant hustle.

But, guess what?

It worked.

I remember the students, myself included, feeling almost giddy with delight upon our second and third encounter with our new Department Chairman. He now had us right where he wanted us, and he played us all like a banjo.

He'd hoodwinked us with the be strong – be good reversal, which very few of us saw coming.

Although there will be infrequent occasions when you will find this technique being employed, it is good to be able to recognize it when it appears to be in play. You will find when you're able to identify it, you'll also be able to temper your enthusiasm for the person or the ideas that are being sold to you.

That is not to say that you are to resist anyone or any presentation where this strategy is employed. It's just that once you do recognize it to be in play, you'll be able to draw conclusions much more objectively, rather than be seduced by the strategy itself. You'll be able to maintain an open-minded view of the subject matter without being inadvertently influenced by the tactic the speaker is employing.

Again, you may infrequently find yourself on the receiving end of this strategy since it is a rather arcane one. However, you may find this technique very useful when *you* are able to use it on your audience.

This strategy is a good change-up to pitch when your opponent appears to harbor preconceived ideas or obstinate views on the subject matter. Be strong – be good may gently jostle the mind set of your opponent to a more receptive open-minded forum.

Since the strategy is usually unexpected, it often gives you the chance to clear the way of any residual ideas or preconceptions, and then, start fresh. You'll find the appreciation of the fresh, new look that is unveiled to be eagerly embraced.

This strategy works especially well on children.

Children are especially adept at taking advantage of adults, and they are often quick to abuse a good thing. When faced with little or no consequences, children will often behave incontinently. However, with specified consequences in place, the little angels will often behave as such.

As reluctant as I am to admit it, I employed this tactic when I coached in Little League and with children's soccer teams.

At the beginning of each year, I was typically faced with a considerable amount of new faces staring up at me on that first day of practice. I would begin the first session a deliberate stern edge. I would rarely refer to the children by their first names. In most cases, I couldn't do so anyway since I'd yet to learn their names. I'd bark rather than speak to them.

I would lighten-up a bit during the second session. When I'd speak or refer to a player, I'd do so only by his or her last name. I'd somewhat soften my previously hard edge, but I'd still remain a distant and aloof adult figure.

By session three, I'd become a kinder and gentler figure. I'd project a much more upbeat, positive, and warm image to the kids. I'd speak to them more softly, and when I would speak or refer to any one of them, I'd always do so by their first names. I'd anchor the good and warm feelings with smiles, happy faces, and pats on the back, or touches on the arm.

The kids always responded especially strong to the change. It seemed that their respect was dramatically increased by the evolution of kindness. Perhaps it was the utter relief that they weren't being coached by Ivan the Terrible that spurred their respect. But I do believe that their subconscious appreciation of the goodness of the situation, which evolved before their very eyes, is what they embraced with such open arms.

It may sound crazy to be utilizing psychology and management techniques on little children. But, I must confess, it works in an overwhelming majority of cases.

Try this technique for yourself, even if it's only on your own children. Then, study it and its results. You'll be pleasantly surprised with its effectiveness.

LESSON TWENTY-THREE

Grow old and grow wise

Senior citizens are a very valuable resource to society. As they grow older their acquired knowledge makes them even more valuable. The wealth of knowledge that they've amassed through their lives cannot be rivaled or duplicated by any school or textbook. There is no substitute for experience, and experience can be a very persuasive element in any conversation or debate.

Experience, however, is an under utilized persuasive tool in many communication exchanges in this country. The North American society today is very influenced by the "new and improved" mentality, and there is an inclination to appeal to the interests of the "young generation."

America is a young country by world standards, and it lacks the history and cultural nuances handed down through the ages that permeate the societies of many European and Asian countries. In contrast, the Japanese, for example, are an old-world society. They embrace their senior citizens and their input eagerly. The input of their seniors weaves a valuable texture to an ancient culture, which continues to grow through the generations, like additions to an ever-in-progress patchwork quilt that is intertwined to their very fabric of life.

The power of experience is strong and its persuasive influence is equally powerful.

The lesson here is: Do not overlook the value of experience in communication. It maybe be somewhat overlooked, but it is still a very potent persuasive tool.

Empower yourself to think positively about your own aging process and look to leverage your own acquired experience as a tangible advantage in instances where you can gain an advantage by utilizing your own experience as an example to strengthen your argument..

In 1937, a man named Napoleon Hill wrote a book titled, *Think and Grow Rich!* The book sold over ten million copies and has influenced many – including Andrew Carnegie and Dr. Norman Vincent Peale – over the decades since its release.

Hill, also, served as an advisor to Franklin D. Roosevelt. In fact, it was Hill who gave Roosevelt the idea for his famous speech, "We have nothing to fear but fear itself."

Hill firmly believed that experience was a great teacher. He associated wisdom and personal wealth with acquired experience. Among his conclusions was, the older you live to be, the wiser you become. With your accumulated wealth of wisdom, your value to yourself and your society increases. Furthermore, your value and wisdom renders you a very persuasive person in instances where you can apply your experience.

Never stop trying to grow, and you will continue to do so. And, never cease to attempt to interject your personal experience to a debate or conversation where it may be appropriately applied.

For example, in 1984, Ronald Reagan ran for reelection – at the tender age of seventy-six – against a much younger candidate. Through the presidential debates, Reagan consistently projected himself to be a much better prepared candidate. During TV debates, Reagan constantly called on his on-the-job experience as president when he answered the questions posed to him. His opponent was at a considerable disadvantage since he had no presidential experience and could speak in only hypothetical terms to the questions presented to him.

The voters found Reagan to be the much more persuasive of the two – he won reelection by a landslide.

Utilize your experience and apply it to communication instances where it can enhance your persuasiveness. Do not underestimate its value as a communication tool.

Nothing on this planet is more convincing and persuasive than the words of wisdom coming from somebody who's already been there.

LESSON TWENTY-FOUR

Putting it all together

The objective of this book is to help its reader become a more persuasive communicator, and, also, to help its reader resist being overwhelmed by an excessively convincing opponent.

Hopefully, it has been informative in addition to being somewhat entertaining.

This book has established that building rapport will tremendously increase your own persuasiveness. Also, being able to recognize the many subliminal communication techniques, that are being employed by persuasive speakers, will help you avoid being persuaded at inappropriate times – otherwise known as being bullshitted.

Take your time to study many of the techniques described in the preceding pages. Read, and reread them until you feel you have fully understood and mastered their theroies and principles.

Then, just for the fun of it, go ahead and imagine your own "dream" negotiation situation.

Your boss schedules your year-end review. He arranges the meeting to take place in your office – giving you the home-field advantage – at 8:00 AM tomorrow morning – he is not a morning person. As he enters your office, you touch him on the arm as you tell him how nice the suit he is wearing looks – you set your anchor. You know him to be a kinesthetic person and you begin mirroring him both physically and verbally. Soon you are pacing him, and before long, you are leading.

At the end of the review, you thank him as you touch him on the arm. Suddenly, he turns to you and announces that it is you who should be giving the review and not him. He continues to tell you how much smarter you are than him and he agrees to exchange jobs and salaries with you.

You agree with him. Then, in a gesture of kindness, you give him the rest of the day off.

He thanks you, shakes your hand, and leaves what will soon be his new office.

Is this too good to be true?

Probably.

But, you can dream, can't you?

LESSON TWENTY-FIVE

And, the best part is, they won't have a clue!

Once you have read, and then, re-read this book, you can begin to actively apply the lessons discussed to your everyday affairs.

Study, practice, and then begin to work the lessons into you activities, be it at work or at play. Start slowly, but then build-up the intensity of the exercises you employ. Don't try to accomplish too much too soon or it won't work for you. Go slowly and begin to master the skills you learn one-at-a-time.

Become a good listener and practice that skill with diligence. As simple as it may appear to be, acquiring good listening skills is difficult for most. Many people have so much to say that they view the listening part as merely a pause in their own delivery of words. Don't think that way. You can learn much more from listening than you can from speaking. Let others do the talking – you do the listening. When you have acquired a sufficient amount of information, then and only then, should you carry on with your own dissertation on the subject at hand.

Develop a way with words. This doesn't mean you need to become a skilled orator, but mark out key phrases and persuasive statements that you can incorporate into you own working vocabulary. Increase the power of your vocabulary by reading and listening to persuasive speakers. Mark out the key words or phrases that they use to make or emphasize their persuasive points. Embrace those phrases as your own and massage them into your own working vocabulary. Keep a keen eye out for clever or even humorous phrases.

I have a friend who stands about five-feet, two-inches tall. He is, by all accounts, a short individual. His diminutive size may be a handicap for him in certain situations. He is aware of this. However, where his height – or lack thereof – may sometimes be an obstacle for him, he is quick to reverse the negative into a positive. He readily admits that, in physical height, he is somewhat lacking. But he doesn't refer to himself as "short." Instead, he classifies himself as "vertically challenged." And, he is quick to tell you this.

In almost every situation where his height may be an issue, my friend disarms his opponent with this self-analysis. His personal assessment always draws a respecting smile and his size handicap, in nearly every situation, becomes a moot point.

Next, always try to follow the theories in this book when communicating. Try to negotiate on your home-field, study your opponent's home-base of communication, speak to them in that mode, and mirror and image your subject when possible. Try to put every known advantage to your benefit when communicating. Leverage every technique studied to your advantage.

I recently had a gentleman come to me about buying my company. He was from a company that is about ten times the size of mine, so it was very conceivable that he could, in fact, acquire my firm.

His first mistake was he agreed to meet me at my office. There, he relinquished the home-field advantage. I told him when to arrive, where to meet me, and even where to sit when he got there. I totally controlled the negotiation setting.

I soon recognized him to be a kinesthetic by his words and eye movements. I began to answer him in his own mode of communication. I felt he sensed a strong rapport building between us when I answered him in his terms. I said things like, I *grasped* his reasoning for acquisitions. He understood me when I spoke to him in this fashion.

I mirrored his physical movements as he sat before me in his chair. When he crossed his legs, I did likewise. He put his right hand in his pocket as he spoke. I did the same on my cue to talk. This went on and on, down to the fact that he nervously cleared his throat and drew his clenched fisted to his mouth before he had something important to say. I did the very same when I told him I wasn't interested in selling. He accepted my answer readily without a rebuttal. He understood me too well. I led him where I wanted him to be and he followed without hesitation.

Do you know what?

It was all too easy. He didn't know what hit him. He was a very intelligent guy, but he didn't stand a chance. He didn't have a clue as to what I was doing to him.

And that's the beauty of this. Nearly everyone on whom you employ these techniques will not know they are being manipulated and led. Only you will know what's going on. It's the ultimate sting. You win, and the competition doesn't even know they lost.

What could be better?

You win, they lose, and they don't even know it. There is not a better negotiation or communication situation in the world.

Why?

Because it allows you the opportunity to win, and win again against opponents who don't know what you are doing, and haven't even a clue as to how you are doing it.

Enjoy the advantage – it's yours.

ABOUT THE AUTHOR

Gerry Borreggine is the President of 40 Winks Sleep Shops, a nationally recognized chain of mattress stores, located in the Philadelphia market. Many of the communication techniques outlined in this book have been practiced and developed on the sale floor of the retail stores he operates.

Gerry also serves on the Board of Directors of the Better Sleep Council, a non-profit, consumer information organization whose mission is to educate the public about the benefits of a good night's sleep. He is the President of the organization.

Gerry, along with his wife, Regina, daughter, Kristin, and son, Kyle, make their home in the Philadelphia area.